SIZE, GROWTH, AND U.S. CITIES

SIZE, GROWTH, AND U.S. CITIES

Richard P. Appelbaum

PRAEGER PUBLISHERS
Praeger Special Studies

New York • London • Sydney • Toronto

900

PRAEGER PUBLISHERS
PRAEGER SPECIAL STUDIES
383 Madison Avenue, New York, N.Y. 10017, U.S.A.

Published in the United States of America in 1978
by Praeger Publishers,
A Division of Holt, Rinehart and Winston, CBS, Inc.

89   038   987654321

© 1978 by Praeger Publishers

Library of Congress Catalog Card Number: 78-61885

Printed in the United States of America

To Mask, Ruby, and their
many friends and relatives—
Urban Expatriates All

the project. The theoretical considerations raised in Chapter 8 reflect his influence, as well as that of the members and visitors to his graduate seminar on urban sociology, particularly Greg Allain, Becky Cannon, John Gilderbloom, and Marsha Sato. Bill Bielby, Roger Friedland, and Sandy Jencks—all of the UCSB Sociology Department—also provided me with invaluable comments and advice on theoretical matters, as did David Harvey, of the Geography Department at Johns Hopkins University. Final responsibility for the book lies, of course, entirely with its author.

CONTENTS

SIZE, GROWTH, AND U.S. CITIES

The optimal size of urban settlements has probably been
debated since the earliest sedentary societies found different
families living in proximity to one another. In the fifth
century B.C., Plato called for the division of the city into
5040 lots, each housing a citizen—the maximum number
Plato felt could participate in face-to-face governance in the
public amphitheatre.[1] Aristotle apparently felt this to be too
large in number and territory for the adequate pursuit of
"the enjoyment of leisure," and, therefore, limited his ideal
city to 10,000 persons of all classes (Mumford 1961:172,
185). In recent years there has been a growing concern in the
United States over the consequences of population growth on
urban living. Numerous cities and suburbs have attempted to
restrict growth through population ceilings, rezoning, building permit bans, and moratoria on sewer and water hookups;
one source estimates that as many as 200 communities and
regions in the United States were taking or considering taking
action to limit growth in 1974 (Finkler and Peterson 1974:
18-19). The Department of Housing and Urban Development
estimates that over one-third of the cities and suburbs in the
United States have been affected in one way or another.

THE ISSUE OF GROWTH

Until very recently, "growth" has been a part of the conventional wisdom of U.S. urban and economic folklore, strongly buttressed by market economic theory. Sociologists and economists alike argue that population growth, economic development, and the elimination of poverty go hand-in-hand (for example, see Wallich 1972; Passel and Ross 1972). The readers of *Newsweek*, the *New York Times Magazine*, or any textbook in urban economics will find ample documentation for their belief that "bigger is better." The argument may be couched in terms of necessary minimal thresholds for self-sustaining urban economic development (Thompson 1965: 24; Clark 1945), optimal trade-offs in a free market economy (Mills and de Ferranti 1971), or simply the hard-nosed recognition that in our economy "growth is a substitute for equality of income," since "so long as there is growth, there is hope, and that makes large income differentials tolerable" (Wallich 1972:62). Economic growth and population growth are identified with one another and as opposed to the environmental movement. The latter's advocacy of "nongrowth" is seen as ill-informed utopianism at best, and—more likely—a cruel, middle-class hoax whereby the recently arrived middle classes "kick the ladder down behind them,"[2] in what Alonso (1973:194) terms a "beggar-thy-neighbor strategy." Thus formulated, environmental concern is conceptualized in terms of "trade-offs" with necessary economic growth; the choice of less affluent Americans, presumably, is clearly in favor of continuing economic (and, hence, population) growth. Urban planners have traditionally conceived of themselves as accommodating to growth rather than planning to control it; the standard textbooks of the planning profession do not even consider no-growth as a serious planning policy (for example, Chapin 1965; this argument is made strongly in Finkler 1972:788). It appears, then, that "the growth ethic is so deeply engrained in our values that nothing less than a 'basic recasting of American values' would be needed to slow growth" (Finkler 1972:5, quoting from *U.S. Commission on Population and the American Future* 1972:18–19).

However deeply engrained it may be, the "growth ethic" is presently under attack on many fronts. While the ecology movement has been most conspicuous in this regard, the argument has been joined by economists, political scientists, planners, blue-ribbon commissions, and citizens' groups in many communities. The limits of world population and economic growth were analyzed in the well-known Club of Rome study (Meadows, Randers, and Behrens 1972); economists such as Herman Daly have recently argued for the necessity of a "steady-state" approach to economics at the national level, with concomitant emphasis on redistribution of existing wealth (see, for example, many of the articles collected in Daly 1972; Wilson 1977, Pirages 1977; Johnson 1973). One international association of activists and social scientists, the New York based Institute for World Order, boasts a growing "steady-state network" of some 100 persons concerned with developing alternative models to unlimited growth and developing educational programs around those alternatives. A major study of the dangers of continued growth in the United States was recently completed by the U.S. Commission on Population Growth and the American Future (1972); its conclusions—which occupy seven volumes—detail the hazards of depending on technological and administrative solutions to growing population pressures (see, for example, the introduction to volume III, "Population, Resources, and the Environment"). An issue of the journal *Daedelus* (1973) was devoted entirely to the controversies surrounding "the no-growth society." Even the planner's traditional pride in being able to "cope with growth" is currently coming under attack within the profession itself; as planners become involved in local controversies over growth, many are coming to seriously consider "non-growth as a planning alternative."[3]

METHODOLOGICAL LIMITATIONS OF GROWTH-IMPACT STUDIES

While much of the debate over growth has been at the national level, the consequences of growth are experienced locally—often in the form of higher taxes, increasing traffic congestion and air pollution, and social costs of various sorts. Many communities—particularly middle-sized communities in growing metropolitan areas—have thus moved in the past few years to limit growth through land-use measures. Such growth-control policies, while basing themselves in the presumed costs of growth, seldom result from an understanding of the dynamics of growth or even from a systematic comparative study of costs and benefits. As a result, growth-control policies are often reactive, parochial, and based on inadequate theories and poor information—and have met with mixed receptions in the courts. While a number of comparative studies on the effects of city size have been conducted in this century, they have tended to employ widely diverging criteria for assessing the impacts of growth. Furthermore, data bases are often not truly comparable—with some studies focusing on large metropolitan areas, others on small towns, and most on incorporated cities irrespective of their relationships to surrounding urbanized areas. While some body of consistent findings has resulted, it is not clear how these findings can be generalized.

There are two purely methodological deficiencies that characterize most existing studies of the correlates of urban size. First, there is a notable lack of uniformity in the meaning of urban, reflected in units of analysis that include cities, counties, SMSAs, and census-defined urbanized areas. Inasmuch as overlapping political jurisdictions, common employment and market areas, and shared environment characterize many adjacent municipalities, the unquestioned reliance on geopolitical units determined by the immediate requirements of data collection minimally introduces at least random measurement error into the analysis—and possibly serious bias as well (for instance, if smaller units tend to be suburban). It would appear that a definition of urban should be more systematically related to the dependent variables of interest, rather than merely derived on an ad hoc basis from available data. A second deficiency is the lack of comprehensiveness of existing studies. By focusing on a single variable or group of variables, one loses the ability to draw conclusions concerning the combined social, economic, and political effects across the same set of urban areas. This difficulty is compounded by the wide variation in definitions and methodologies employed in the various studies.

The present research, in an effort to overcome such difficulties, reconsiders earlier studies in light of an analysis of the correlates of size and growth for a comparable set of places across a number of social and economic measures, including indicators of economic conditions, crime, health, and public expenditures. It will thus permit comparisons to be made and trade-offs among various variables to be estimated.

THEORETICAL CONSIDERATIONS

The principal shortcomings of growth-impact studies are not methodological, however; they are, rather, theoretical in nature. Instead of departing from explicit theoretical models of the dynamics of urban growth, most studies remain at the descriptive level, analyzing the social, political, and economic correlates of population size and increase. This is due to a combination of two factors: the underdeveloped state of urban theory and the political context within which studies are generally conducted.

The task of a theory is to abstract from the numerous and seemingly accidental properties of observable phenomena those which are important in understanding their behavior. A good theory tells us which aspects of a phenomenon are interesting, and which are not; it suggests a conceptual framework or "map" with which to view the phenomenon in question; and it further suggests correct ways in which to operationalize concepts for the purpose of testing the theory against empirical observation. Most studies of urban growth are unabashedly empiricist. The question they address— "what are the effects of growth"—does not grow out of a body of theory which suggests such a question might be important; rather it results from practical considerations, principally the requirements of policy planning. The meaning of "growth" is therefore uninformed by theoretical con-

siderations; rather, it is dictated by the practical requirements
of urban planners and urban economists. The former customarily deal with questions of urban land use. For such
planners, growth is taken to mean an increase in the number
of people on urban land, either through spatial extension,
densification, or some combination of the two; the demographic variables are then treated as causing other processes.
Thus, for example, an increase in population on limited
urban land entails crowding, traffic congestion, and, therefore, higher levels of friction between people; these in turn
are seen to result in increased social disorganization (for
example, higher crime levels) and personal stress (for
example, higher rates of mental illness). On the other hand, a
spatial extension of population—for example, through
suburbanization—is regarded as resulting in greater depend-
ence on the automobile, with such readily observed consequences as extended commuting times and higher levels of
vehicular air pollution. While such observations may appear
self-evident, in the absence of a theory, they actually tell us
very little about the underlying processes involved—and,
therefore, very little about the actual meaning of growth.
What, for example, is the significance of densification?
Crowding depends on the patterns of land use, not simply on
the number of people per acre; extremely high acreage densities are compatible with a spacious living environment, as
high-rise luxury condominiums demonstrate. Traffic congestion is the result of mode of transportation, as well as the
volume of people to be moved; a viable public transportation
system—or a commitment to bicycles—may permit considerably higher densities than does the private automobile. The
effects of physical crowding on social or individual pathology
vary widely from society to society; clearly, sheer number of
people is not the whole story. Suburbanization need not
entail long automobile commutes and consequent pollution,
if it is paralleled by industrial decentralization and rigid pollution control. In each instance, the population variable masks
less apparent or altogether unknown processes that are in fact
primary. Such processes determine whether increased population will mean densely packed tenements or urban villages,

a metropolitan agglomerate linked by freeways or some other form based on economic decentralization and public transportation, or an urban life characterized by friction and pathology or one characterized by neighborliness and cooperation.

Urban economists face a similar set of difficulties. They assume that economic processes are fundamental, and therefore construct models in which the economic variables are causal. So, for example, an urban economist seeking to explain the consequences of growth might construct an economic base model, in which sectoral interdependencies are formally represented by equations drawn on the basis of past observations. Economic growth in one sector—which may be treated as an exogenous variable—will then be seen to ramify throughout the economy; through the use of economic and population multipliers, the future shape of the economy and the population can be anticipated. Such an approach is perhaps more explicit in its use of modeling than that of the urban land-use planners, but it also exhibits empiricist tendencies: the models limit themselves to observable economic variables, leaving *ceteris paribus* those underlying forces which, in fact, shaped the sectoral interdependencies on which the econometrics are based. Perhaps this is why in one case with which I am directly familiar, a seemingly well-conceived econometric base analysis overestimated the growth of a California county by 100 percent over a mere ten-year period (Appelbaum et al. 1974: 6-7). The forces determining economic growth in that county were not adequately understood and, therefore, not adequately incorporated into the econometric model.

In both of these instances—urban land use and urban economic approaches to growth—the problem is the same: theoretical considerations are subordinated to those of policy making. The land-use planner thinks in terms of zoning and densities; most policy tools deal with numbers of establishments, or dwelling units, or people on parcels of land. It is, therefore, not surprising that studies commissioned by land-user planners should emphasize the causal nature of demographic variables. Similarly, urban economists think in terms

of job expansion and commercial growth; their recommenda-
tions are often couched in terms of improving the "business
climate," making an area more attractive to outside investment. Their studies, therefore, emphasize the importance of
stimulating economic growth, treating all other processes as
secondary. In neither case is there a direct concern with the
development of theory itself; the theories which result are
often elaborate rationales for simple inductively derived
models.

I shall return to the issue of urban theory in chapter 8,
where I will raise some suggestions concerning the direction
which theory formation might take. For the present, however, it is necessary to note that the present research suffers
from the limitations just described. This book grew out of a
growth-impact study commissioned by the city council of a
California community in 1974; the explicit purpose of that
study, under the terms of the agreement between the city
and the task force that completed it, was to evaluate the
effects of population and economic growth in anticipation of
an eventual revision of the city's zoning and general plan. The
study was to become a planning document—a basis for decid-
ing on eventual growth-management policies. While the bulk
of the analysis consisted of a case study of the impacts of
growth on the city itself,[4] it was also felt that comparative
information was necessary; data was therefore collected and
examined for a comparable set of urban places. A limited
analysis of this data was reported in the initial study (Appelbaum et al. 1976: ch.2); the present study consists of a re-
analysis of the data, employing more powerful multivariate
techniques. But it must be kept in mind that the data were
initially collected with an eye to policy planning, under
severe time and financial constraints, and subject to con-
tractual arrangements which effectively restricted analysis to
issues that had a practical payoff for planners concerned with
the effects of growth per se. In other words, the initial study
did not approach the dynamics of urban growth from the
standpoint of the development of theory; nor was a body of
theory available which might have directed the collection of
data. Rather, the study sought simply to examine the consequences of growth from a land-use planning standpoint, in

light of the findings of previous studies which had addressed the same issue from the same perspective. Because of this initial concern, the data generated proved to be ill-suited for the subsequent testing of theory. I have, therefore, not attempted to use the data to test causal models of urban growth. Rather, a procedure is employed which seeks to disentangle size and growth effects from other variables, which are likely involved in the dynamics of growth, in order to suggest the underlying processes for which size and growth constitute crude indexes. It is recognized that this approach can merely be suggestive—that the most that can be hoped for is some greater clarity in understanding the nature of urban growth, an understanding which will contribute to the eventual articulation of an explicit theory. Only then will it be possible to conduct a study that will reveal and test the processes of real scientific interest.

OVERVIEW OF THE BOOK

In the following chapter, I shall discuss the overall approach of the study—the units of analysis, the variables employed and their operationalization, and the methodological procedures to be utilized. These procedures are further explicated in chapter 3, where they are applied to the analysis of the private sector economy. In that chapter I shall examine the impacts of size and growth on such variables as family income, cost of living, the concentration of poverty, income inequality, unemployment, and general economic structure. Chapter 4 considers more conventional sociological indicators, including various measures of public health and crime. Chapter 5 then turns to an examination of the public sector—the effects of size and growth on the size and cost of governmental services. A sixth chapter departs from the comparative analysis, briefly reviewing previous studies which have attempted to specify the relationship between urban growth and the physical environment, and which have examined popular attitudes toward city size. Chapter 7 summarizes the findings of the study, and then returns to the more theoretical concerns raised earlier in this chapter. The concluding chapter reconsiders the entire notion of growth effects, in light of an emerging theoretical framework which seeks to locate urban development within larger societal processes. It offers some speculations on an underlying dynamic which accounts for both size and growth, and the associated effects.

NOTES

1. Mumford (1961:180) estimates this would produce an actual population of twenty-five or thirty thousand persons, since the land-holding guardian caste of male and female citizens would be supported by perhaps a thousand warriors and many times that number of servitors.

2. A phrase employed in a Mobil Oil advertisement that appeared in the *New York Times*, 17 February 1972, p. 37. The Mobil Oil Company at that time ran a series of advertisements to counter the rising environmental movement and convince the public that growth is a prerequisite for the elimination of poverty. One ad states:

> GROWTH IS THE ONLY WAY AMERICA WILL EVER REDUCE POVERTY. . . . While the relative share of income that poor people get seems to be frozen, their incomes do keep pace with the economy. It's more lucrative to wash cars or wait on tables today than 20 years ago. . . . Twenty more years of growth could do for the poor what Congress won't do (quoted in Johnson 1973:168).

3. This is the title of a planning-oriented monograph by Finkler (1972); he notes that an unpublicized session under the same name at the 1972 annual meetings of the American Society of Planning Officials drew some 150 persons. The 1974 annual meetings of the American Institute of Planners attracted over 2,700 persons around such themes as resource conservation and growth management (see *A.I.P. Newsletter* 9:12, December 1974). Similarly, the Northeast regional meetings of the Urban Land Institute (Spring 1975) focused on issues in no-growth. For a recent analysis of the no-growth movement in urban planning, see Finkler and Peterson, 1974.

4. The study looked at both the public and private economies, as well as social, environmental, and physical impacts of growth in Santa Barbara, California; it was conducted under a grant from the City Council.

THE STUDY: ANALYZING SIZE AND GROWTH
IN 115 COMPARABLE U.S. URBAN PLACES

Most U.S. cities have grown in a haphazard fashion. As is well known, urban agglomerations often embrace numerous governmental entities and overlapping jurisdictions. Contiguous cities usually constitute a single area from an economic point of view, with employment opportunities, housing markets, commerce, and industry shared by all residents of the area. Furthermore, it is often the case that cities will "specialize," with one jurisdiction providing jobs and related economic services, while a neighboring one is largely limited to residential development. Residents of adjacent cities share the same highways and traffic congestion, breathe the same air, deplete the same water resources, and face similar problems of waste disposal. It generally makes little sense to compare cities themselves, inasmuch as such comparisons are confounded by historical and political developments that are not systematically related to city size.

Yet on the other hand, the incorporated city as a legal entity is the locus of most governmental services. Whatever the degree of specialization of the city, almost all cities are charged with the responsibility of providing police and fire protection, highway maintenance, parks and recreational facilities, and often water and sanitation services. The costs of such services are borne by the residents of cities, however far they may commute for their daily needs and regardless of the degree to which such services are consumed by those who reside elsewhere. So in making certain comparisons among cities—those having to do with public expenditures and revenues—it is necessary to respect political boundaries.

UNITS OF ANALYSIS

Most studies have ignored these difficulties, gathering data for incorporated cities regardless of their functional role within larger urban agglomerations, although a few have looked at SMSAs, and some have attempted to aggregate municipal expenditure data for all cities within the county. The present research seeks to avoid these problems by restricting its analysis to a limited range of urban places—those of medium size and relative "self-containment." I look at all U.S. cities[1] and their surrounding urbanized areas[2] that satisfy two criteria: (1) there is a single central city with a 1970 population of 50,000 to 400,000 people; and (2) the central city is at least 20 miles from the closest neighboring urbanized area. I exclude cities that are exclusively bedroom communities (or play some other specialized role in the context of a larger metropolitan area) as well as the very smallest places—on the assumption that all such places may have unique characteristics and problems that complicate comparisons. It should be noted that the places studied are in many ways typical of the places that most Americans who reside in SMSAs experience. According to the *1970 Census of Population* (U.S. Dept. of Commerce 1973a: sec. 2:1-44), 26.8 percent of all Americans live in cities of 50,000 to 500,000 people; only 15.6 percent live in larger cities, while the remainder (over half the population) live in smaller places, unincorporated towns, and rural areas. The largest city in the analysis (Toledo, Ohio) ranked 34th among all U.S. cities in size in 1970 that is, there are only 33 cities excluded from consideration purely because they have too many people.

There are 115 places that meet the two criteria.[3] It should be emphasized that these places are not simply a sample; they constitute all such places in the continental United States.[4]

VARIABLES EMPLOYED IN THE ANALYSIS

I am primarily interested in knowing whether size and growth are systematically related to various indicators of urban life. In most studies reviewed, these two effects are confounded; it is my intention to disentangle them. To estimate the effects of size I compare the 115 urbanized areas at a single point in time—that of the 1970 census. For certain economic indicators, I employ urbanized area population as the measure of size. This reflects the fact that income, employment, poverty, and the housing market are all best conceptualized as characterizing entire urban areas rather than a single political entity within such areas. For all other indicators, on the other hand, city population is the measure utilized. To estimate the effects of growth I look at the population change for the urbanized area during the period 1960–1970. City growth rate was not used as an independent variable because it proved to be misleading; almost all growth experienced by cities was due to annexation of adjacent areas.

Dependent variables are conceptualized as indicators of various aspects of urban life that are affected by changes in the size and rate of growth of the population. Results are reported for four different sets of such indicators, summarized in Table 2.1. Dependent variables are converted either to per capita terms, or are expressed as median figures. Those dependent variables which are expressed in per capita terms are mathematically related to the independent variable— population size—the former having been standardized on the latter.[5]

TABLE 2.1

Urban Life Indicators Used in the Analysis

I. The Private Economy—Provision of Goods and Services to the Private Sector (Urbanized Area)
   1. Median family income
   2. Percentage of families below federal poverty level[a]
   3. Index of income inequality[d]
   4. Rate of unemployment
   5. Median house value[b]
   6. Median gross rent[c]

II. Crime (City)[e]
   7. Murders and homicides per 10,000 residents
   8. Robberies and burglaries per 10,000 residents
   9. Automobile thefts per 10,000 residents

III. Public Health (City)[f]
   10. Deaths from bronchitis, emphysema, and asthma per 10,000 residents
   11. Deaths from cirrhosis of the liver per 10,000 residents
   12. Motor vehicle deaths per 10,000 residents
   13. Suicides per 10,000 residents
   14. Infant deaths per 10,000 residents [g]

IV. The Public Sector (City)[h]
   15. Per capita expenditures on fire protection
   16. Per capita expenditures on police protection
   17. Total number of common function personnel per 10,000 residents[i]
   18. Total payroll on common function personnel per capita

Notes

a.   The poverty cutoff point is determined "by such factors as family size, sex of the family head, and the number of children under 18 years old . . . at the core of this definition of poverty is a nutritionally adequate food plan." (U.S. Dept. of Commerce 1973a: App.–32)

b.   "Value is the respondent's estimate of how much the property (house and lot) would sell for if it were for sale. . . . The statistics on value are . . . only for one-family houses on less than ten acres without a commercial establishment or medical office on the property." (U.S. Dept. of Commerce 1972: App.–11)

c.   Gross rent "is the contract rent plus the estimated average cost of utilities . . . and fuels. Thus, gross rent is intended to eliminate the differentials which result from varying practices with respect to the inclusion of utilities and fuel as part of the rental payment." (U.S. Dept. of Commerce, 1972: App.–11)

d.   This measure is derived from the Lorenz curve; it varies from 0 to 1. As it approaches 0, income is increasingly equally distributed; for example, 5 percent of the families will possess 5 percent of the total income, 10 percent of the families 10 percent of the income, and so on.

e.   Crime statistics are "number of offenses known to police" by place of occurrence in each year. They are available for cities only.

f.   Vital statistics are by place of residents and in each year. They are available for cities only.

g.   "Infant death" means "born alive but died within one year."

h.   Figures are for cities only.

i.   "Personnel" here refers to full-time equivalent employees. This, in turn, is the "number of full-time employees" plus "total expenditures for part-time employees divided by the average expenditure for a full-time employee." "Common functions" include police and fire protection, wastewater and sanitation, parks and recreation, and water supply.

Source: Compiled by the author.

METHOD OF ANALYSIS

The analysis involves a cross-sectional study of the relationship between size and growth rate and indicatiors of urban life among 115 places in 1970, utilizing Multiple Classification Analysis (MCA).[6] MCA is a technique for simultaneously assessing the variables on a dependent variable. Under the strategy adopted in the present study, one first tests the data for interactions among the predictors (in this case, the techniques and programs recommended in Sonquist et al. 1971 were employed). In the absence of interaction effects an MCA is then performed to disentangle intercorrelations. Independent or predictor variables are conceptualized as consisting of two kinds: explanatory and test factors.

The two independent variables—population size and growth rate—were divided into categories to serve as explanatory factors. Population size was divided into quintiles such that approximately one-fifth of the urban areas fell into each category. Growth rate was divided into three categories—one representing negative growth (anything under 10 percent over the decade),[7] one representing moderate growth (10-25 percent), and one representing rapid growth (25 percent or greater). Again, about one-third of the urban places fell into each category.

The test factors employed in the study are presented in Table 2.2. These nine variables were derived from a larger list of variables which were thought to possibly affect the relationship between size, growth, and any of the dependent variables. They represented every underlying dimension found to differentiate cities according to Hadden and Borgatta's (1965) comprehensive factor analysis of 65 variables on 644 U.S. cities, along with several additional variables related to economic structure. The final test factors employed in the reported results are those which proved to be significantly related to the dependent variable in question ($p \leqslant 05$), when included in a regression equation with all other independent variables. (It should be noted that the test factors, unlike the explanatory factors, are all linearly related to the dependent variables.) When the test factors are employed in the analysis of the economic indicators, they refer to the entire urbanized area; for all remaining indicators, test factors refer to cities (refer to Table 2, note a).

PROCEDURAL CONSIDERATIONS

As indicated in the introductory chapter, I am not attempting in this book to specify a causal model of urban growth. Inasmuch as there is little in the extant literature to warrant such modeling, I have adopted the more restrictive standpoint of the urban policy planner who is concerned to know, simply, the likely correlates of size and growth, once other factors are taken into account. Accordingly, I employ the following procedure in assessing the relationship between size, growth, and the various indicators of urban life. First, I measure the separate effects of size and growth on each indicator. Next, I estimate their conjoint effects, so as to disentangle the contribution of each. Finally, I estimate the effects of size and growth net of the influence of associated test factors. Therefore, apart from the distinction between explanatory and test factors, I make no further distinctions among independent variables, nor do I draw detailed theoretical inferences from the relative size of coefficients.

SOURCES OF DATA

A detailed inventory of sources of data keyed to each variable is contained in Appelbaum et al. (1974, vol.3:11–20); bibliographic information is provided at the end of this book. All information comes from several principal sources. Basic demographic housing and governmental data is from the *U.S. Census of Population* (U.S. Dept. of Commerce 1973a, 1973b), *City Governmental Finances* (U.S. Dept. of Commerce 1961b, 1970), *City Employment* (U.S. Dept. of Commerce 1961a, 1971), *The U.S. Census of Housing* (U.S. Dept. of Commerce 1963a, 1972), and the *County and City Data Book* (U.S. Dept. of Commerce 1962, 1973b). Data on

TABLE 2.2

Test Factors Used in the Analysis

I. Characteristics of cities or urbanized areas[a]

1. Age of city (number of decades since census in which central-city population surpassed 50,000)

2. Region (dummy variable taking on a value of "1" if the city is located outside the South, and "0" if not)[b]

3. Percent of housing units in single-family structures

4. Population density

5. "Metropolitan consolidation" (central-city population as a fraction of total urbanized area population)

II. Characteristics of the population

6. Median family income[c]

7. Median age

8. Median adult schooling

9. Percent of population that is black or of Spanish-American descent[d]

Notes

a.   In the analysis of the private economy, all variables—size, growth, test factors (where appropriate), and the six economic indicators—refer to the entire urbanized area. In the remaining analyses (crime, health, and public sector), data for the indicators were available only for cities; as a consequence, both "size" and test factors (where appropriate) refer to cities exclusively. "Growth" continues to refer to the entire urbanized area, however, for reasons given in the text.

b.   "South"—a 0-score on this variable—includes the following states: Texas, Oklahoma, Arkansas, Louisiana, Kentucky, Tennessee, Mississippi, Alabama, West Virginia, Virginia, North Carolina, South Carolina, Georgia, and Florida.

c.   This variable is employed both as a dependent variable and, in conjunction with other dependent variables, as a test factor.

d.   According to the *1970 U.S. Census of Population,* "in 42 states [the population of "Spanish" heritage] is identified as 'persons of Spanish language'; in five southwestern states, as 'persons of Spanish language or Spanish surname'; and in the three middle-Atlantic states, as 'persons of Puerto Rican birth or parentage.'" In the present study, the percentage of black or "Spanish heritage" is summed into a single variable.

Source: Compiled by the author.

health are taken from *Vital Statistics of the United States, Volume II* (U. S. Dept. of Health, Education and Welfare 1963, 1973). Crime data is obtained from the FBI's *Uniform Crime Reports* (U.S. Dept. of Justice 1961, 1971). Additional information is found in the *Municipal Year Book* (International City Management Association, 1961, 1972). It should be noted that the data sources used in this analysis are very numerous and disparate. There are quite possibly inconsistent methods of record keeping and data compilation across cities. The effect of such inconsistencies is to introduce disturbance into the pattern field, thus inhibiting the discovery of actual relationships. The findings should be regarded as conservative estimates of actual relationships.

NOTES

1. "A political subdivision of a state within a defined area over which a municipal corporation has been established to provide local government functions and facilities." (U.S. Dept. of Commerce 1973a.)

2. "A central city or cities, and closely settled territory." Ibid.

3. The 115 places included in the analysis are: Abilene, Texas; Albany, Georgia; Alburquerque, New Mexico; Altoona, Pennsylvania; Amarillo, Texas; Ann Arbor, Michigan; Asheville, North Carolina; Augusta, Georgia; Austin, Texas; Bakersfield, California; Baton Rouge, Louisana; Billings, Montana; Binghamton, New York; Birmingham, Alabama; Boise City, Idaho; Boulder, Colorado; Cedar Rapids, Iowa; Charleston, South Carolina; Charleston, West Virginia; Charlotte, North Carolina; Chattanooga, Tennessee; Colorado Springs, Colorado; Columbia, South Carolina; Columbus, Georgia; Corpus Christi, Texas; Decatur, Illinois; DesMoines, Iowa; Dubuque, Iowa; Erie, Pennsylvania; Eugene, Oregon; Evansville, Indiana; Fayetteville, North Carolina; Flint, Michigan; Fort Smith, Arkansas; Fort Wayne, Indiana; Fresno, California; Gadsden, Alabama; Gainesville, Florida; Great Falls, Montana; Green Bay, Wisconsin; Greenville, South Carolina; Harrisburg, Pennsylvania; Huntsville, Alabama; Jackson, Mississippi; Kalamazoo, Michigan; Knoxville, Tennessee; La Crosse, Wisconsin; Lafayette, Louisiana; Lake Charles, Louisiana; Lancaster, Pennsylvania; Lansing, Michigan; Las Vegas, Nevada; Lawton, Oklahoma; Lexington, Kentucky; Lima, Ohio; Lincoln, Nebraska; Louisville, Kentucky; Lubbock, Texas; Lynchburg, Virginia; Macon, Georgia; Madison, Wisconsin; Mansfield, Ohio; Mobile, Alabama; Modesto, California; Monroe, Louisiana; Montgomery, Alabama; Ogden, Utah; Orlando, Florida; Owensboro, Kentucky; Pensa-

cola, Florida; Peoria, Illinois; Pine Bluff, Arkansas; Pittsfield, Massachusetts; Portland, Maine; Pueblo, Colorado; Reading, Pennsylvania; Reno, Nevada; Richmond, Virginia; Roanoke, Virginia; Rochester, Minnesota; Rockford, Illinois; Sacramento, California; Saint Joseph, Missouri; Salem, Oregon; Salt Lake City, Utah; San Angelo, Texas; Santa Barbara, California; Santa Rosa, California; Savannah, Georgia; Shreveport, Louisiana; Sioux City, Iowa; Sioux Falls, South Dakota; South Bend, Indiana; Spokane, Washington; Springfield, Illinois; Springfield, Missouri; Springfield, Ohio; Stockton, California; Syracuse, New York; Tacoma, Washington; Tallahassee, Florida; Terre Haute, Indiana; Toledo, Ohio; Topeka, Kansas; Tucson, Arizona; Tulsa, Oklahoma; Tuscaloosa, Alabama; Tyler, Texas; Waco, Texas; Waterloo, Iowa; West Palm Beach, Florida; Wichita, Kansas; Wichita Falls, Texas; York, Pennsylvania.

4. For a discussion and justification of the use of statistical tests of significance when the units of analysis constitute a universe rather than a sample, see Gold 1969.

5. We are aware that correlations among ratio variables such as these pose certain conceptual problems, but have adopted the practice in keeping with the conventions of past studies of this sort (for discussions of these difficulties, see Fuguitt and Lieberson 1974; Schuessler 1974).

6. For a detailed discussion of this technique, see Sonquest et al. 1971; Andrews et al. 1973; Blau and Duncan 1967: 128-40; and Smith 1975. We have employed MCA because, unlike multiple regression analysis, it makes no assumptions concerning linear relationships between explanatory and independent variables. Many studies of the effects of urban growth have in fact reported a U-shaped curve to characterize growth and size effects (for example, with regard to per capita levels of public expenditures).

7. Ten percent was employed as the upper limit for "negative growth" because under the fertility patterns of the period, any urban area that did not grow at a minimal rate of 1 percent per annum (the approximate rate of natural increase) was likely losing population through outmigration.

3

SIZE, GROWTH, AND
THE PRIVATE SECTOR

In this chapter I examine the relationships among growth, size, and various measures, including income, poverty, income inequality, unemployment, and housing.

MEDIAN FAMILY INCOME

Numerous studies have found that average per capita income is higher in larger places. Most analyses have found a positive correlation between population and mean or median income (Oliver 1946; Duncan and Reiss 1959; Schnore and Varley 1955; Ogburn and Duncan 1964; ACIR 1968), although one study—by examining correlations within major size categories found this to be true only in the largest metropolitan areas (Hadden and Borgatta 1965:112). One study that attempted to control for variations in the composition of the labor force across cities was Fuchs' (1967) analysis of 1960 census hourly earnings data. In examining the effect of city size on earnings, Fuchs controlled for what he termed quality or composition of the labor force—operationalized as differences in race, sex, age, and educational attainment. He also controlled on region, since he was particularly interested in seeing if the large south-nonsouth differential could be attributed to quality differences.[1] Fuchs found that even after standardizing on his control variables, a substantial hourly earning differential remained that could be attributed to city size; "The relation between earnings and city size is large, persistent, and cannot be explained by the correlation between city size and other variables" (Fuchs 1967:31). He estimated that standardized hourly earnings were typically 25-35 percent higher in SMSAs of one or more million persons, in comparison with areas outside of SMSAs, and about 15 percent higher than in SMSAs of fewer than one million. Fuchs also noted that the city-size gradient was steeper in the South than elsewhere, and that the persistent city-size differential is not due to the higher costs of living in larger cities, which are alleged to be small relative to the observed wage differences (Fuchs 1967:34). This conclusion is echoed by Hoch (1972a:235-42) and Alonso (1973:197-98).[2]

The present analysis found significant size and growth effects on median income, although the magnitude of such effects is relatively small, particularly when the effects of associated test factors are considered. Table 3 summarizes the results. I shall consider this table in some detail, as the analysis of subsequent variables will closely parallel that of median incomes.

In Part I of Table 3.1 one first notes the mean values of median family income for each of the five categories of urbanized area size and the three categories of urbanized area growth rate. (The unequal n's in each category are due to missing data for dependent variables and test factors.) The column of "unadjusted means" is simply the raw, unweighted average for each category. It is apparent that there is a substantial difference in median income with respect to both size and growth. The difference between the smallest and largest quintile of urbanized areas is $1,012 ($9,854 minus $8,842), while the difference between "negatively growing" and "rapidly growing" areas is $897 ($9,833 minus $8,936). The magnitude of these effects is given by *eta*, which is the simple correlation of the predictor with the dependent variable;[3] its square, reported in Part II of the table, is a measure of the total variance explained by the predictor. In this case, 10.9 percent of the variance in median family income is explained by urbanized area size alone, while about the same amount (10.2 percent) is explained by growth.

The column labled "means adjusted for explanatory factors" presents the average for each predictor category controlling for the effects of the other predictors. The means in this column thus represent the estimates of the effect of a predictor category under the statistical assumption that the other predictor variable is distributed within that category exactly as it is for the total sample (Smith 1973:227). Comparing these means, one notes a slight attenuation of effect of each predictor: the maximum categorical difference for size has declined by about one-fifth to $807, while that for growth has declined by about one-quarter to $651. This is because size and growth are slightly correlated (r equals .12); under the assumptions of the MCA the effects of such intercorrelations among predictors are removed. The column labled "means adjusted for both explanatory and test factors" displays the results of simultaneously controlling on the other explanatory factor, along with the two test factors that were found to be significant predictors of median family income in the multiple regression analysis. We can see that the effect of size is not substantially altered beyond that noted when growth was taken into account; the same is true for growth. A comparison of the eta^2 and $beta^2$ statistics provides a summary of these effects. *Beta* is a partial-correlation measure analagous to *eta*, but based on the adjusted means (see Bachman 1970:70; Andrews et al. 1973:47-49; Smith 1973:234). The adjusted correlation of size with median family income (*eta*) is .33; this drops to .24 (*beta_E*) when the other explanatory factor (growth) is taken into account, and remains at about the same level when the other explanatory factor and the two test factors are simultaneously controlled (*beta_ET*). The corresponding figures for growth are .32, .23, and .18. Apparently, then, a substantial part of the independent effects of urbanized area population size and growth on median family income is due to the conjoint effects of the other variable; together, size and growth account for 15.4 percent of the variance. The introduction of

TABLE 3.1

Effects of Urbanized Area Population and Urbanized Area Rate of Growth, and Selected Test Factors, on Urbanized Area Median Family Income ($)

PART I: Mean Values of Explanatory Factor Categories

Grand Mean = 9386
Grand Standard Deviation = 1116
Total Number of Cases = 110

Explanatory Factor	Number of Cases	Unadjusted Means	Means Adjusted For:	
			Explanatory Factors	Explanatory and Test Factors
POPULATION				
50,000–80,000	14	8842	8938	9018
80,000–125,000	20	8944	9114	9000
125,000–175,000	24	9508	9488	9566
175,000–275,000	25	9608	9512	9507
275,000–400,000	17	9854	9745	9710
Association:		$eta^a = .33$	$beta_E{}^b = .24$	$beta_{ET}{}^c = .25$
Significance of F:d		$p_F = .026$	$p_F = .049$	$p_F = .036$
GROWTH RATE '60–'70				
"negative" (<10%)	31	8936	9047	9112
moderate (10%–25%)	36	9363	9391	9405
rapid (25% and above)	33	9833	9698	9622
Association:		$eta^a = .32$	$beta_E{}^b = .23$	$beta_{ET}{}^c = .18$
Significance of F:d		$p_F = .005$	$p_F = .013$	$p_F = .077$
(100) · MULTIPLE R^2 =		—	15.4	54.6

PART II: Summary Statistics, Explanatory Factors

	Measure of Association			Marginal Variance Added:[e]	
				Each expl. factor, net of other	Expl. factors, net of test factors
Expl. Factor	$(100) \cdot eta^2$ [a]	$(100) \cdot beta_E^2$ [b]	$(100) \cdot beta_{ET}^2$ [c]	ΔR^2	ΔR^2
POPULATION	10.9	5.8	6.3	5.2	} 12.2
GROWTH RATE	10.2	5.3	3.2	4.5	

PART III: Summary Statistics, Test Factors

Test Factor	b[f]	Significance (p_{F_b})[g]
Region	1278	.001
Median Adult's Schooling	470	.078

Marginal Variance Added, Test Factors Net of Explanatory Factors[h] $\Delta R^2 = 39.2$

For Notes to Tables, see page 49.
Source: Compiled by the author.

the test factors serves to further reduce the influence of the explanatory factors by a small amount. The test factors themselves clearly exert substantially more influence than the two principal explanatory variables, since their inclusion raises the total variance explained to 54.6 percent.

Part II of Table 3.1 presents the summary statistics for the MCA. The numbers in the first three columns are the squares of the raw and partial correlation coefficients; they roughly correspond to the proportion of variance explainable in terms of the adjusted means in the corresponding model.

In Part III of the table one can also note the separate effect of each of the two test factors, when the effects of size, growth, and the remaining test factors are simultaneously taken into account. Of all the predictors, "region" is by far the most important single source of differences in median family income; urbanized areas outside of the South have, on the average, median family incomes that are almost $1,300 higher than do southern ones, when differences in size, growth, and education are taken into account. This difference, it will be noted, is substantially greater than that previously observed for size and growth. Median adult education in the urbanized area is also strongly associated with median family income (the zero-order correlation between the two is .48); each unit increase in median education is associated with approximately $500 increase in median family income.[4]

What is the relative contribution of each explanatory factor and the two test factors considered together? There is no single answer to this question (Blau and Duncan 1967: 128–40; Smith 1973:246–55; Bachman 1971:71–75). In Part II of the MCA table we provide several different measures of the relative effects of size, growth, and the test factors on the dependent variable. A maximum estimate of size and growth effects is given by eta^2; this represents the "raw" effect of each variable, obtained without consideration of the other variables; it, therefore, assumes no intercorrelations among predictors. $Beta^2$ is an intermediate measure of effects; $beta_E^2$ estimates each explanatory factor effect controlling on the other, while $beta_{ET}^2$ estimates each explanatory factor effect controlling on the other explanatory factor as well as all test factors. A minimal estimate of effects is given by the marginal variance added (ΔR^2), which is presented for each explanatory factor net of the other, both explanatory factors together net of all test factors, and all test factors net of both explanatory ones. This latter estimate assumes that a given predictor asserts its influence only after all other predictors in the model have already done so.

With respect to median family income, then, one may conclude that size and growth effects are small and of comparable magnitude; together they account for only about 15 percent of the total variance in the dependent variable. Inclusion of two test factors in the model increases the explanatory power to almost 55 percent; the effect of size and growth net of these two variables is reduced to only about one-eighth of the total variance.

A NOTE ON COST-OF-LIVING DIFFERENTIALS

These results actually overstate the effects of size and growth on income to the extent that cost-of-living differentials favor smaller places over larger ones. Several studies have found this to be the case. The cost of housing, for example, is found to increase with size (Hoch 1972b:315-17; Schnore and Varley 1955:413)—although Hadden and Borgatta (1965:112) find this to be true only in the largest places. The Advisory Commission on Intergovernmental Relations (ACIR) report (1965:51) concludes that a "moderate standard of living" costs progressively more in larger urban areas, the simple correlation between family budget and city size being estimated at .37. The most comprehensive studies have produced somewhat contradictory findings, indicating that cost-of-living differences—should they exist—are indeed small relative to income differences. Shefer (1970) reviewed Bureau of Labor Statistics (BLS) studies which attempted to standardize budgets for three livings standards (low, moderate, and high) across 11 expenditure items, for a sample of 39 SMSAs grouped into four geographical regions. Controlling on budget level and region, he found no correlation[5] between size and cost-of-living, with the exception of those places located in the South: in that region only, several of the prin-

cipal items in the low standard budget were found to be more
costly in larger places, and both the low and moderate family
consumption costs increased with size. When all SMSAs were
compared, irrespective of region, no relationship between size
and cost of living was observed. Shefer concludes that "by
and large, no significant relation exists between population
size of an SMSA and the consumer expenditure necessary for
a given standard of living" (1970:420). Hoch (1972a,
1972b), using the same 1966 BLS cost-of-living studies,
employed a regression analysis to predict cost of living as a
function of both region and population. His equation—which
accounted for two-thirds of the variance in cost of living—
found both a significant regional effect (lower costs in the
South), and a modest increase due to size. The difference
between the smallest places (below 50,000) and metropolitan
areas of 1,000,000 or more was over 5 percent in all regions
(1972a:240; 1972b:310-11).[6] He then deflated the wage
rates previously estimated by Fuchs, employing his cost-of-
living differential, by region; the expected result was that
wages remain correlated with size even after cost-of-living differences are taken into account (1972a:241-42). For
example, the "adjusted" income differential between places
smaller than 10,000 and those larger than 1,000,000 ranges
from 7 percent in the Northeast to 29 percent in the South.
The differences among moderately sized places (50,000 to
375,000) can be estimated from his Table 3.2 (Hoch 1972a:
241) as follows:

TABLE 3.2

Percent Differences between Cities of 50,000 and 375,000,*
Average Income, after Adjusting for Cost-of-Living
Differences

Region			
Northeast	North Central	South	West
−2.7	+7.2	+10.8	+1.3

*Midpoints of ranges 10,000–100,000 and 250,000–500,000.
Source: Derived from Hoch 1972a, Table 3:241.

It is clear from Hoch's analyses that for moderately sized places, average incomes do not differ substantially once cost-of-living differences are taken into account. This is especially true in the Northwest and the West, the two most populous regions in the country. Hoch's recent estimate (1976: 193) is that cost-of-living differences (based on goods and services sold) account for one-half to three-quarters of the wage differential with size, while most of the remainder can probably be attributed to "unconventional" costs entailed by increased travel time on congested streets and highways, air pollution, noise, and so forth. These results further reduce the importance of size as a source of real income differentials. It is clear, therefore, that neither size nor growth plays a major role in income differentials among the urbanized areas studied, particularly relative to regional differences and differences in the educational level of population.

While the present analysis did not directly address the issue of cost-of-living differences between urbanized areas, the analysis of housing costs provides indirect evidence, insofar as housing is a main component of the index. Both median house value and median monthly gross rental rates are considered.

Table 3.3 summarizes the results of the MCA with respect to median house values. There appears to be no significant systematic relationship between reported house value and urbanized area size, particularly when growth is taken into account. The pattern of means fluctuates when the various size categories, with a modest eta^2 (10.9 percent) declining to nonsignificant $beta^2$ values when growth and the test factors are introduced. Growth itself exerts a moderate effect independently of size ($beta_E^2$ equals .27); the estimated mean house value for rapidly growing urbanized areas is almost \$4,000 greater than that for those areas losing population, and about \$2,300 greater than for moderately growing areas. Together, size and growth account for almost one-third of the variance in this variable. This pattern lends support for the hypothesis that growth places pressure on the existing housing supply, thereby bidding prices up substantially. Once growth pressures have tapered off, however, housing costs do not vary systematically with the overall level of population

TABLE 3.3

Effects of Urbanized Area Population and Urbanized Area Rate of Growth, and Selected Test Factors, on Urbanized Area Median House Value
($)

PART I: Mean Values of Explanatory Factor Categories

Grand Mean = 15,413
Grand Standard Deviation = 3,094
Total Number of Cases = 100

Explanatory Factors	Number of Cases	Unadjusted Means	Means Adjusted For:	
			Explanatory Factors	Explanatory and Test Factors
POPULATION				
50,000–80,000	14	14,350	15,022	14,464
80,000–125,000	20	13,815	14,833	14,863
125,000–175,000	24	15,925	15,791	15,561
175,000–275,000	25	16,364	15,743	15,868
275,000–400,000	17	16,047	15,427	15,964
Association:		$eta^a = .33$	$beta_F^b = .13$	$beta_{ET}^c = .18$
Significance of F:		$p_F = .026$	$p_F = .232$	$p_F = .124$
GROWTH RATE '60–'70				
"negative" (< 10%)	31	13,339	13,489	14,668
moderate (10%–25%)	36	15,144	14,183	15,460
rapid (25% and above)	33	17,654	17,471	16,061
Association:		$eta^a = .56$	$beta_E^b = .52$	$beta_{ET}^c = .18$
Significance of F:[d]		$p_F = .001$	$p_F = .001$	$p_F = .025$
(100) · MULTIPLE R^2 =		—	33.2	78.9

PART II: Summary Statistics, Explanatory Factors

Measure of Association

Expl. Factor	$(100) \cdot \text{eta}^2$ [a]	$(100) \cdot \text{beta}_E^2$ [b]	$(100) \cdot \text{beta}_{ET}^2$ [c]	Marginal Variance Added: [e] Each expl. factor, Expl. factors, net net of other of test factors ΔR^2	ΔR^2
POPULATION	10.9	1.7	3.2	1.8	⎱ 8.4
GROWTH RATE	31.4	27.0	3.2	22.3	⎰

PART III: Summary Statistics, Test Factors

Test Factor	b [f]	Significance (p_{F_b}) [g]
City age	-38	.001
% Units in Single-Family Structures	-193	.001
Median Family Income ($)	1	.001

Marginal Variance Added, Test Factors net of Explanatory Factors[b] $\Delta R^2 = 45.7$

For notes to Tables, see page 49.
Source: Compiled by the author.

TABLE 3.4

Effects of Urbanized Area Population and Urbanized Area Rate of Growth, and Selected Test Factors, on Urbanized Area Median Gross Rent ($)

PART I: Mean Values of Explanatory Factor Categories
    Grand Mean = 99.10
    Grand Standard Deviation = 18.53
    Total Number of Cases = 100

Explanatory Factor	Number of Cases	Unadjusted Means	Means Adjusted For:	
			Explanatory Factors	Explanatory and Test Factors
POPULATION				
50,000–80,000	14	87.79	92.37	92.19
80,000–125,000	20	92.00	97.75	98.14
125,000–175,000	24	98.71	97.84	96.83
175,000–275,000	25	105.60	101.72	101.94
275,000–400,000	17	107.76	104.15	104.95
Association:		$eta^a = .39$	$beta_E{}^b = .20$	$beta_{ET}{}^c = .22$
Significance of F:[d]		$p_F = .004$	$p_F = .003$	$p_F = .007$

34

GROWTH RATE '60-'70

"negative" (< 10%)	31	87.87	89.01	95.15
moderate (10%-25%)	36	95.22	95.73	96.35
rapid (25% and above)	33	113.88	112.25	105.81
Association:		$eta^a = .59$	$beta_E^b = .52$	$beta_{ET}^c = .26$
Significance of F:d		$p_F = .001$	$p_F = .001$	$p_F = .001$
(100) · MULTIPLE R² =		—	37.8	81.2

PART II: Summary Statistics, Explanatory Factors

	Measure of Association			Marginal Variance Added:[e]	
				Each expl. factor, net of other	Expl. factors, net of test factors
Expl. Factor	$(100) \cdot eta^2{}^a$	$(100) \cdot beta_E^2{}^b$	$(100) \cdot beta_{ET}^2{}^c$	ΔR^2	ΔR^2
POPULATION	15.2	4.0	4.8	3.0	} 10.2
GROWTH RATE	34.8	27.0	6.8	22.6	

PART III: Summary Statistics, Test Factors

Test Factor	b^f	Significance $(p_{F_b})^g$
City age	-.17	.001
Region	4.76	.033
% Units in Single-Family Structures	-.54	.001
Median Family Income ($)	.01	.001

Marginal Variance Added, Test Factors net of Explanatory Factors[h] $\Delta R^2 = 43.4$

For Notes to Tables, see page 49.
Source: Compiled by the author.

achieved, as equilibrium is reestablished between supply and demand in the housing market.

Three test factors substantially reduce the observed relationship between growth and housing value, reducing the $beta^2$ to .03. Housing values are higher in urbanized areas with relatively "younger" central cities, areas which are characterized by apartments rather than single-family structures, areas with relatively higher median family incomes. While it is perhaps tempting to conclude that young, "dynamic" communities accomodate to rapid growth through the construction of apartments, such a conclusion is not warranted on the basis of the data at hand. It is also possible that the lower housing values in older places reflects the predominance of older and less expensive single-family units in such places, rather than the dynamics of growth per se. Similarly, while the analysis suggests that increase in median family income is associated with a comparable increase in median housing value, the reason for this is not clear: while it is possible that people in wealthier communities are willing to spend more on housing, it is also possible that communities characterized by expensive housing attract wealthier immigrants.

One may conclude that while housing values appear to be higher in rapidly growing urbanized areas, this observed relationship is explained in large part by the associated effects of the three test factors, it is possible to account for a substantial 79 percent of the variance in median housing value; while the marginal variance added by the explanatory factors net of the test factors is only 8.4 percent, that of the latter net of the former amounts to 45.7 percent. Consistent with Shefer's earlier findings, size itself is unimportant as a source of variation in housing costs.

Median gross monthly rents exhibit a pattern similar to that of median house value (see Table 3.4). The adjusted effects of growth are considerably greater than those of size ($beta_E^2$) equals .04 and .27 respectively), presumably for the same reasons that housing value was found to be higher in rapidly growing areas. Together, size and growth account for about 38 percent of the variance in median monthly rent; the variance contributed by the latter (net of size) is about 23 percent. The introduction of the test factors reveals that a good part of the effect of size and growth can be attributed to the associated effects of region, central-city age, and such urbanized area characteristics as percentage of housing in single-family dwellings and median family income (rentals are estimated at $4.76 per month lower in southern cities, when size, growth, and the remaining three test factors are controlled). Again, it is not possible to specify which effects are antecedent. All factors together account for over four-fifths of the variance in median gross rents; the contribution of size and growth, net of the test factors, is only 10.2 percent, while that of the test factors, net of size and growth, amounts to 43.4 percent. It should be noted, however, that substantial differences by size as well as growth remain, even after all effects are taken into account. The difference between the smallest and largest places amounts to some 14 percent ($92 vs. $105 in Part I, column 4), while that between moderately growing and rapidly growing places is about 10 percent.

In sum, with respect to housing as one major component of the cost of living, one may conclude that both housing values and monthly rentals are higher in rapidly growing urbanized areas, while rentals are higher in larger areas regardless of growth. These patterns persist, although moderated, when the associated effects of the test factors are taken into account.

POVERTY

Both Alonso (1973:198) and Richardson (1973:52-54) have argued that the proportion of families living in poverty declines as size increases—although because of their increasing numbers and concentration, the poor may become more visible. Alonso offers no evidence for his assertion, while Richardson bases his conclusions on various other studies, and qualifies them by observing that "the most marked and dramatic change takes place at the very top [population levels]" (1973:53). In Table 3.5 one finds partially supporting evidence for this proposition.

TABLE 3.5

Effects of Urbanized Area Population and Urbanized Area Rate of Growth, and Selected Test Factors, on Urbanized Area Poverty (percent of families below federal poverty level)

PART I: Mean Values of Explanatory Factor Categories

Grand Mean = 10.40

Grand Standard Deviation = 4.04

Total Number of Cases = 96

Explanatory Factor	Number of Cases	Unadjusted Means	Means Adjusted For:	
			Explanatory Factors	Explanatory and Test Factors
POPULATION				
50,000–80,000	11	11.80	11.57	10.71
80,000–125,000	20	10.61	10.39	10.37
125,000–175,000	23	10.12	10.14	10.26
175,000–275,000	25	10.80	10.98	10.81
275,000–400	17	9.03	9.16	9.82
Association:		$eta^a = .20$	$beta_E{}^b = .18$	$beta_{ET}{}^c = .09$
Significance of F:[d]		$p_F = .108$	$p_F = .001$	$p_F = .269$

38

GROWTH RATE '60-'70

"negative" (< 10%)	31	10.84	10.70	10.77
moderate (10%–25%)	33	10.70	10.73	10.38
rapid (25% and above)	32	9.66	9.76	10.06
Association:		$eta^a = .13$	$beta_E{}^b = .11$	$beta_{ET}{}^c = .07$
Significance of F:^{d}		$p_F = .212$	$p_F = .020$	$p_F = .329$
$(100) \cdot$ MULTIPLE $R^2 =$		—	5.0	86.7

PART II: Summary Statistics, Explanatory Factors

Expl. Factor	Measure of Association			Marginal Variance Added:^{e}	
	$(100) \cdot eta^2{}^a$	$(100) \cdot beta_E{}^{2\ b}$	$(100) \cdot beta_{ET}{}^{2\ c}$	Each expl. factor, net of other ΔR^2	Expl. factors, net of test factors ΔR^2
POPULATION	4.0	3.2	0.8	3.3	} 1.0
GROWTH RATE	1.7	1.2	0.5	1.0	

PART III: Summary Statistics, Test Factors

Test Factor	b^f	Significance $(p_{Fb})^g$
Region	-1.32	.004
Median Family Income ($000)	-1.88	.001
% Black or Spanish-American	.07	.001
Median Age	- .29	.001
Median Adult Schooling	-1.08	.044

Marginal Variance Added, Test Factors net of Explanatory Factors^h $\Delta R^2 = 81.7$

For Notes to Tables, see page 49.   *Source:* Compiled by the author.

Looking first at the column of unadjusted means, one sees that 2.77 percent more families live in poverty in the smallest quintile of urbanized areas than the largest; a smaller difference obtains between places losing population and those growing rapidly (1.18 percent). The two effects are largely independent of one another, as a comparison of means (or of *eta* and *beta$_E$*) between columns 1 and 2 suggests. While both size and growth effects are statistically significant, they are substantially quite small; together, they account for only 5 percent of the variance in the poverty variable. In addition to the two explanatory factors, five test factors were found to be significantly related to "poverty" in the regression analysis region, median family income, percent black or Spanish-American, median age, and median adult schooling (all variables refer to urbanized areas). Together with the two explanatory factors, they account for 8.6 percent of the total variance. The marginal contribution of the explanatory factors net of the test factors is estimated at only 1 percent; the inclusion of the test factors in the model reduces the effects of size and growth to nonsignificance.

One may conclude, therefore, that size and growth effects on poverty are minimal when these two variables are considered by themselves; when considered in conjunction with the associated variables they are no longer important.

INCOME CONCENTRATION

Alonso (1973:198) has argued that income distribution does not vary systematically with size. Betz (1972) has also found this to be the case, when differences among places in industrial diversification, income level, and racial composition are taken into account. Consistent with these studies, the present one does not find a significant association between urbanized area size or growth and this measure of the maldistribution of income.

UNEMPLOYMENT

There is conflicting evidence on the relationship between official local unemployment rate[7] and size, although the majority of studies find no relationship tetween the two (Samuelson 1942; Levy and Arnold 1972:95; Sierra Club, San Diego 1973:21–30; Molotch 1976). Hadden and Borgatta (1965:108) found no relationship between official unemployment rates in 1960 and size among places smaller than 150,000. The average rate in that year was about the same (5 percent) for their three smaller city-size categories (25,000-50,000, 50,000-75,000, 75,000-150,000). While they found rates to be somewhat higher (5.4 percent) in cities over 150,000, this may be due to the different ecological structure of larger, older cities; if political boundaries fail to expand as a city grows, the more affluent and stable working populations may move outside the city limits, leaving the central core to industrial uses and the underemployed and unemployed. The difficulty here is the one mentioned previously—that of taking the politically delimited city for the unit of analysis, rather than the urban unit as a whole. Other studies have produced ambiguous results. Duncan and Reiss (1956: 95), for example, found higher unemployment rates in urban areas of over one million, with no systematic relationship between unemployment and size in smaller places; Flaim (1968), however, found no relationship among the 20 largest places (all over a million). One study of British cities over 50,000 in 1956 (Vipond 1974; reviewed in Richardson 1973:63-64) concluded that unemployment increases with size for males, whereas for females it declines to a low point in places of around 500,000, rising thereafter.

There is apparently little agreement in terms of previous studies on which to base any conclusions concerning the empirical relationship between size and place and unemployment. There are, however, some theoretical reasons for expecting the absence of any strong relationship. While any area may have its own unique reasons for experiencing a given level of unemployment in the short run (for example, the closing down of an industry of major economic importance to the area), in the long run, rates will tend to fluctuate

TABLE 3.6

Effects of Urbanized Area Population and Urbanized Area Rate of Growth, and Selected Test Factors, on Urbanized Area Rate of Unemployment
(percent)

PART I: Mean Values of Explanatory Factor Categories

Grand Mean = 4.44
Grand Standard Deviation = 1.44
Total Number of Cases = 100

Explanatory Factor	Number of Cases	Unadjusted Means	Means Adjusted For:	
			Explanatory Factors	Explanatory and Test Factors
POPULATION				
50,000–80,000	14	4.49	4.59	4.06
80,000–125,000	20	4.46	4.50	3.92
125,000–175,000	24	4.29	4.27	4.38
175,000–275,000	25	4.34	4.28	4.45
275,000–400	17	4.74	4.72	5.43
Association:		$eta^a = .11$	$beta_E{}^b = .12$	$beta_{ET}{}^c = .34$
Significance of F:[d]		$p_F = .999$	$p_F = .999$	$p_F = .028$
GROWTH RATE '60–'70				
"negative" (< 10%)	31	4.43	4.43	4.86
moderate (10%–25%)	36	4.28	4.25	4.17

rapid (25% and above)

    Association:

    Significance of F:[d]

(100) · MULTIPLE R^2 =

PART II: Summary Statistics, Explanatory Factors

Expl. Factor	Measure of Association			Marginal Variance Added:[e]	
				Each expl. factor, net of other	Expl. factors, net of test factors
	$(100) \cdot eta^2$ [a]	$(100) \cdot beta_E^2$ [b]	$(100) \cdot beta_{ET}^2$ [c]	ΔR^2	ΔR^2
POPULATION	1.2	1.4	11.6	1.5	} 9.3
GROWTH RATE	1.0	1.4	4.0	1.3	

PART III: Summary Statistics, Test Factors

Test Factor	b [f]	Significance (p_{F_b}) [g]
City age	- .022	.002
Region	1.681	.001
Median Family Income ($000)	- .502	.002
Median Age	- .136	.005

Marginal Variance Added, Test Factors net of Explanatory Factors[h] ΔR^2 = 34.1

For Notes to Tables, see page 49.
Source: Compiled by the author.

around national or perhaps regional unemployment levels. This is true to the extent that the labor force is mobile. An economic slowdown means that persons will emigrate, while, conversely, economic expansion means that persons will be attracted. The key issue is one of the distribution of jobs at the national level and not the creation of jobs locally; a locality can capture a plant or a university from a competing city, and the associated jobs along with it, but it cannot create "new" jobs (see Molotch 1976). Thus, should a city seek to solve its unemployment problem through job creation, it will in the long run attract persons from elsewhere who are seeking work, and the local jobless rate will remain about the same —although the absolute size of the unemployed population will increase (Appelbaum, et al. 1976:123-28).[8]

The results of the present analysis are ambiguous with respect to those of previous studies. In Table 3.6 one notes that neither size nor growth is significantly related to the rate of unemployment, either independently or when the effects of the other are taken into account. Together, size and growth account for only 2.5 percent of the variance in the rate of unemployment. Four test factors were, however, found to be significantly associated with unemployment when considered in conjunction with size and growth: age of the central city, region, urbanized area median family income, and median age of the urbanized area population. These test factors apparently served as suppressor variables, because their inclusion in the model results in a weak association between urbanized area size and the unemployment rate (growth remains unaffected). When the age of the central city, region, urbanized area median family income, and median age of the urbanized area population are considered, the difference between the smallest and largest quintiles of urbanized areas increases to 1.37 percent (5.43 percent-4.06 percent); the principal difference appears to be between places smaller and larger than 275,000. When size, growth, and all test factors are considered, about 37 percent of the variance in the rate of unemployment is explained; The marginal variance added by the explanatory factors net of the test factors is estimated at 9.3 percent.[9] Looking at Part III of the table, it was noted that the rate of unemployment is higher in areas with "younger" central cities, in areas outside the South, and in areas characterized by lower median incomes and younger populations. One may conclude, therefore, that there is a slight tendency for the rate of unemployment to be slightly higher in the largest quintile of places analyzed, once the associated effects of the test factors are taken into account. Growth, on the other hand, remains unassociated with the rate of unemployment.

A NOTE ON JOBS, INDUSTRIAL BASE, AND GROWTH

While the creation of new jobs does not, in the long run, affect the local unemployment rates, it will foster population growth. This is particularly true if the jobs are in economic sectors which serve external markets—that is, which export goods and import wealth into the community. Such "basic" economic activities are therefore often termed "city-forming" (Bollens and Schmandt, 1965:117). It should be noted that to some extent economic growth and population growth constitute a circular process that is self-sustaining—at least until the costs of growth (social and environmental costs, traffic congestion, higher labor costs, and so forth) begin to outweigh the benefits in the eyes of private firms or local policy makers. The "self-sustaining" nature of growth results from a number of interrelated factors. The location of a new "export" or basic firm in an area has a multiplier effect on local income and jobs, as income generated by the firm is spent locally, thereby stimulating further demand for goods, services, and the associated labor necessary to produce and market those goods and services. Furthermore, as a city grows, "thresholds" in market size are reached, permitting firms with minimum market requirements to locate for the first time in the area; these firms can then provide goods and services which were formerly imported from outside. This "import substitution" further augments the economic activity which triggered it initially. A related advantage of larger cities, from the point of view of some firms, is that they provide for a wide range of business-oriented services (advertising, accounting, marketing, etc.) that permit firms to contract out for services that would be costly to provide by the firm itself. Similarly, finance may be more readily available in larger cities, which possess large local banks willing to extend loans. Other factors associated with large cities that favor ecomomic growth include the presence of a large and presumably heterogeneous labor supply, increasing market demand, and a general atmosphere of "boom," stimulating investment. New firms, jobs, and markets seem to go hand-in-hand: "In cities which have grown rapidly, growth seems to feed upon itself: the location of every new firm appears to add to the attractiveness of the city for still another" (Stanback and Knight 1970:62; see generally pp. 61-73). From the standpoint of the worker, however, such a "growing economy does not necessarily mean a higher likelihood of obtaining a job, for new workers will be attracted proportionally, competition for local jobs will increase as the number of jobs increases, and the relative number of unemployed will in the long run be unaffected. Moreover, the absolute amount of unemployment—reflected, in part, in the geographical concentration of poverty—will become more pronounced.

Many economists have argued that a minimum size or threshold is necessary for a city to guarantee such structural characteristics as "industrial diversification . . . huge fixed investments, a rich local market, and a steady supply of industrial leadership" (Thompson 1965:24); such characteristics "may almost ensure its continued growth and fully ensure against absolute decline—may, in fact, effect irreversible aggregate growth" (Ibid.; see also Clark 1945). Thus, larger cities are viewed as "more efficient engines of production" (Alonso 1973:197), providing opportunities for specialization in services, as well as a heightened atmosphere of innovation and invention (Hoch 1972b:324; Duncan 1951: 771-72). According to this view, "the larger places have a clear and sizeable advantage in such areas as cheaper and more flexible transportation and utility systems, better research and development facilities, a more skilled and varied labor supply, and better facilities for educating and training workers" (Thompson 1968:60). All this serves to lower private costs—while enabling private business to "slough off on society various social costs that its presence imposes, such as its addition to traffic congestion and air pollution" (Ibid.).

There is actually very little known about the dynamics of urban growth; evidence is scanty and does not encourage generalization. Thompson (1974:7) offers a cautionary note, as does Richardson (1973:71-72, 75, 81). While certain types of industrial and financial activity may indeed require a minimum population threshold, this is probably not true for most economic activities and is decreasingly true of manufacturing and light industry—the traditional engines of the growth dynamic. Schnore and Varley found that cities did not differ by size according to the proportion of their labor forces engaged in trade or manufacturing (1955:410-12), although smaller cities tended to be somewhat more retail-oriented (1955:412). While Stanback and Knight (1970), analyzing census data for 1960, conclude that "there are well-defined tendencies for industrial composition of employment to vary according to size of place" (1970:94), they also note that jobs in manufacturing are currently being created at a slower rate in the largest metropolitan areas, "indicating a tendency of industrialization to play a larger role in the growth of smaller places" (1970:114). This, in turn, may be attributed to the increasing tendency of industrial firms to decentralize to nonmetropolitan and suburban areas—where land costs and taxes tend to be low, there is ease of access to the interstate highway system, and social problems are minimal (ACIR 1968:51).

The existing relationship between manufacturing and city size thus appears to be diminishing. For example, Mark and Schwirian (1973:40-41), studying 92 Iowa communities, conclude that "during the period of regional industrialization . . .central-place function was no longer a significant community-building activity"; growth was rather seen to result from such factors as the decentralization of industrial activity (between 1950 and 1960 30 percent of all new plants were located in open country or small towns) and the expansion of institutional facilities such as hospitals, colleges, nursing homes, retirement villages, and penal institutions. Thompson (1974:8) notes that outside the South, there is currently a significant negative correlation between specialization in manufacturing and growth rate. Richardson (1973:78-80), reviewing a study by Hoover (1971) which disaggregated manufacturing into specific types of production, observes that "the most striking features of these results are the large number of industries with a favored city size class in the lower range, the high degree of flexibility in choice of location in terms of city size, and many key industries scattered indiscriminately among all city sizes" (1973:79). Richardson concludes that "the relationship between specialization in specific industries and city size is much more blurred than a priori analysis might suggest" (1973:80).

NOTES

1. Fuchs (1967) does not examine differences in the composition of the labor force by occupation or industry; thus, it is not possible to conclude whether size differences are due to a shift towards higher-income occupations as cities grow. As indicated below, the evidence concerning this is ambiguous. It must also be noted that Fuchs' operationalization of "quality" assumes that such variables as race and sex are indicative of earning ability, rather than reflective of systematic racial and sexual discrimination, particularly when differences of age and education are also taken into account. Fuchs recognizes this difficulty ("The white-nonwhite differences are probably due in part to market discrimination," 1967:5, note 11), but concludes nonetheless that "color is relevant to quality because of the likelihood that, at given levels of education, nonwhites have received poorer-quality schooling and less on-the-job training than have whites" (Ibid.). This justification hardly seems adequate.

2. Hoch also notes (1972b, 313-14) that city-size differences in average income declined steadily during the period 1929–50 and have since stabilized.

3. *Eta* is analogous to r; it is employed when categorical variables are used as predictors. See Bachman 1970:70; Smith 1975:234; Andrews, et al. 1973:7.

4. This relationship must not be interpreted too stringently, inasmuch as education in the census is not coded into equal intervals.

5. Rank-order correlation was performed, and *tau* calculated.

6. Hoch attributes the different results between his study and Shefer's as due to the fact that Shefer "took correlations of ranks of cities and ranks of living costs. It can be inferred that the measures employed obscured the underlying relationships" (Hoch 1972b:310). Presumably Hoch's regression analysis was more sensitive that Shefer's use of rank-order correlations.

7. The difficulties in conceptualizing and measuring unemployment—resulting in severe unemployment and underemployment concealed in the official figures—are well-known. For an excellent discussion of unemployment and underemployment among U.S. workers, see Braverman 1974: ch. 17. Braverman also discusses the problems with conventional measures of social class (parts IV and V).

8. The characteristics of the population may change, however, particularly insofar as migrants tend to be relatively young and well-educated relative to the nonmigrant populations.

9. This figure is greater than the 2.5 percent for the two main effects by themselves because of the strengthening of the relationship between size and unemployment that occurs when the test factors are introduced.

NOTES TO TABLES

[a]*eta* is the correlation coefficient between the explanatory factor expressed as a categorical variable and the dependent variable.

[b]*beta*$_E$ is the partial-correlation coefficient, analogous to *eta* but based on the adjusted means; it is thus a measure of the power of the explanatory factor with all other predictors held constant. The subscript E means that the *beta* is for one explanatory factor, adjusting for the effect of the other; *beta*$_E$ is thus computed at the point where both explanatory factors are in the model, but not the test factors.

[c]*beta*$_{ET}$ is for one explanatory factor, adjusting for the effect of both the explanatory factors and the test factors; it is thus computed at the point where all factors are in the model (that is, the "full model").

[d]p_F is the significance of the F ratio (computed as the ratio of the mean square for the factor in question, divided by the mean square for the residual). F is computed at the point where the factor enters the model. That is, the F for the means of each explanatory factor net of the other is computed on the basis of means adjusted for explanatory factors but not test factors, while the F for means in the "full model" is computed on the basis of means adjusted for all factors.

[e]See text for derivation of ΔR^2.

[f]The unstandardized regression coefficient, the measure of the effect of the test factor in the "full model."

[g]p_{F_b} is the significance of the F-ratio for b in the "full model." Its computation is indicated in note d above.

[h]See text for derivation.

SIZE, GROWTH, AND
THE SOCIAL ENVIRONMENT

There is a weak relationship between city size and such conventional measures of socioeconomic status as income (see previous chapter) and education Schnore and Varley 1955:190-91), although the evidence is mixed (see, for instance, Hadden and Borgatta 1965:107-10). Larger cities tend to have a higher proportion of nonwhite residents (Schnore 1963:189-90; Hadden and Borgatta 1964:107), particularly in the central cities of urbanized areas in recent years.

PUBLIC HEALTH

There is a conventional wisdom that the high population densities associated with large cities are responsible for general social and psychological disorganization—that excessive crowding produces pathological behavior. The existence of "behavioral sinks" has been domonstrated among overcrowded populations of Norway rats (Calhoun 1962), but the generalizability of such studies to human populations is questionable (for an extensive review of studies relating human crowding to pathology that comes to this conclusion, see

Fischer, Baldassare, and Ofshe 1974). Larger cities tend to be
denser than smaller cities (for example, Schnore and Varley
1955:410; Hoch 1972b:309; Hadden and Borgatta 1965:
107, 112), but there is no reason why high densities per se
should induce pathology. Given sufficiently spacious apart-
ment residences, for example, one could achieve very high
densities by building vertically while retaining substantial
privacy in the immediate (home) environment (as an extreme
example, the "arcologies" of Paulo Soleri, or perhaps more
realistically, the John Hancock building in Chicago). Jane
Jacobs has hypothesized that overcrowding (excessive number of persons per residential unit) rather than density (number of persons per unit area) is responsible for many urban
problems (1961:ch. 11; see also Alonso 1973:197), but at
least one study of social disorganization in Honolulu casts
doubt on this hypothesis. Schmitt (1966) studied nine
indexes of health problems and general social disorganization[1] in the Honolulu SMSA during the period 1948–52. He
found a substantial median correlation among all indexes
with density (r = .83), but a much lower one with crowding
(r = .37); furthermore, the density correlation remained high
when crowding was statistically controlled, while the reverse
was not true, leading Schmitt to conclude that "in Honolulu,
at least, population per net residential acre continued to
reveal a close association with morbidity, and social break-
down rates when overcrowding, as measured by the percent
of occupied units with 1.0 or more persons per room, was
held constant" (1966:39). Another study of hospitalized
depressive disorders and suicides in 50 communities near
Boston found that the fastest-growing communities experienced the highest rates (Wechsler 1961). The meaning of such
statistics is anything but clear, however. Persons who are
depressive or suicidal may be attracted to rapidly growing
urban places—just as persons who exhibit behavior conven-
tionally labeled as "disorganized" may, for economic or
other reasons, be forced to live in dense, overcrowded central-
city areas. High rates of disease, infant mortality, and morbidity, in general, are associated with both poverty and race—
and poor nonwhites, unable to afford or obtain quality housing, tend to live in crowded substandard housing in dense

areas of deteriorating city cores. It is not possible to conclude from the available evidence that either density or crowding produce social or psychological disorders in urban populations; rather, it seems likely that economic forces allocate such behaviors (and their labels) to certain segments of the population, while at the same time allocating those segments to crowded and dense portions of the cities. One may conclude that the effect of size and density on health and social problems in general remains ambiguous (Hoch 1972b:320; Hoch 1972a:272-73; Alonso 1973:197; Duncan 1951:762-63), despite their empirical association. On the other hand, health services are probably more extensive in larger cities than in smaller ones; for example, the proportion of physicians to total population (particularly specialists) increases with city size, although differentials may be diminishing (Duncan 1951). Actual access by the poor to health services, however, may be even more limited in the largest cities relative to the smaller ones. In general, the lower infant mortality rates in larger cities may be in large part due to the availability of better facilities.

To the extent that such respiratory ailments as bronchitis, emphysema, and asthma result from air pollution, one might expect a correlation with size if indeed air quality tends to be worse in large places relative to smaller ones. In fact, such health indexes might serve as a partial index of air quality. Motor vehicle deaths per capita presumably should increase in larger places; traffic congestion and travel time increase with city size (Duncan 1951:761-62; Morgan, Sirageldin, and Baerwaldt 1966:80; Hoch 1972a:243). Infant deaths should be lower in large cities to the extent that there is a greater availability of medical services—although not all segments of the population have equal access to such facilities. Cirrhosis might serve as an indicator for stress, insofar as the disease is often associated with alcohoism, and alcoholism, in turn, presumably reflects in part the stressful conditions of daily life. Finally, suicides are presumably an indicator of social disorganization; as previously noted, several studies have found that the rates of suicide and mental disorder are higher in denser areas of cities (Schmitt 1966) or in faster-growing places (Wechsler 1961).

TABLE 4.1

Effects of City Population and Urbanized Area Rate of Growth, and Selected Test Factors, on City Cirrhosis Deaths
(rates per 10,000 population)

PART I: Mean Values of Explanatory Factor Categories

Grand Mean = 15.51
Grand Standard Deviation = 7.73
Total Number of Cases = 77

Explanatory Factor	Number of Cases	Unadjusted Means	Means Adjusted For: Explanatory Factors	Explanatory and Test Factors
POPULATION				
50,000–62,000	5	15.28	14.51	10.42
62,000–75,000	10	16.99	16.78	15.91
75,000–120,000	20	14.12	14.90	16.04
120,000–175,000	23	14.39	14.11	15.45
175,000–400,000	19	17.61	17.43	16.16
Association:		$eta^a = .19$	$beta_E^b = .18$	$beta_{ET}^c = .18$
Significance of F:d		$p_F = .999$	$p_F = .195$	$p_F = .257$
GROWTH RATE '60–'70				
"negative" (<10%)	21	13.37	13.47	11.58
moderate (10%–25%)	25	16.50	16.27	16.22

54

rapid (25% and above)

	31	16.16	16.28	17.60
Association:		$eta^a = .17$	$beta_E{}^b = .16$	$beta_{ET}{}^c = .32$
Significance of F:d		$p_F = .333$	$p_F = .110$	$p_F = .001$
(100) · MULTIPLE R^2 =		—	6.1	66.1

PART II: Summary Statistics, Explanatory Factors

	Measure of Association			Marginal Variance Added:[e]	
				Each expl. factor, net of other	Expl. factors, net of test factors
Expl. Factor	$(100) \cdot eta^2{}^a$	$(100) \cdot beta_E{}^2{}^b$	$(100) \cdot beta_{ET}{}^2{}^c$	ΔR^2	ΔR^2
POPULATION	3.6	3.2	3.2	3.2	⎱ 9.8
GROWTH RATE	2.9	2.6	10.2	2.5	⎰

PART III: Summary Statistics, Test Factors

Test Factor	b^f	Significance $(p_{F_b})^g$
% black or Spanish-American	.304	.001
Median Age	1.623	.001
Region	7.729	.001

Marginal Variance Added, Test Factors net of Explanatory Factors[h] ΔR^2 = 60.0

For Notes to Tables, see page 49.
Source: Compiled by the author.

TABLE 4.2

Effects of City Population and Urbanized Area Rate of Growth, and Selected Test Factors, on City Suicides
(rates per 10,000 population)

PART I: Mean Values of Explanatory Factor Categories
Grand Mean = 13.29
Grand Standard Deviation = 5.65
Total Number of Cases = 77

Explanatory Factor	Number of Cases	Unadjusted Means	Means Adjusted For:	
			Explanatory Factors	Explanatory and Test Factors
POPULATION				
50,000–62,000	5	11.08	11.39	8.63
62,000–75,000	10	16.64	16.44	15.66
75,000–120,000	20	12.49	12.33	13.10
120,000–175,000	23	12.95	12.84	13.69
175,000–400,000	19	13.02	13.68	12.98
Association:		$eta^a = .25$	$beta_E^b = .24$	$beta_{ET}^c = .27$
Significance of F:d		$p_F = .321$	$p_F = .105$	$p_F = .075$
GROWTH RATE '60–'70				
"negative" (<10%)	21	12.72	12.93	12.01
moderate (10%–25%)	25	11.89	11.82	12.27

rapid (25% and above)	31	14.80	14.72	14.98
Association:		$eta^a = .23$	$beta_E{}^b = .22$	$beta_{ET}{}^c = .25$
Significance of F:[d]		$p_F = .138$	$p_F = .043$	$p_F = .036$
$(100) \cdot$ MULTIPLE $R^2 =$		—	11.1	52.2

PART II: Summary Statistics, Explanatory Factors

	Measure of Association			Marginal Variance Added:[e]	
				Each expl. factor, net of other	Expl. factors, net of test factors
Expl. Factor	$(100) \cdot eta^2{}^a$	$(100) \cdot beta_E{}^2{}^b$	$(100) \cdot beta_{ET}{}^2{}^c$	ΔR^2	ΔR^2
POPULATION	6.3	5.8	7.3	5.8	} 12.0
GROWTH RATE	5.3	4.8	6.3	4.8	

PART III: Summary Statistics, Test Factors

Test Factor	b^f	Significance $(p_{F_b})^g$
% black or Spanish-American	.20	.001
Median Age	1.20	.001
Region	2.77	.034
Median Adult Schooling	2.88	.005

Marginal Variance Added, Test Factors net of Explanatory Factors[h] $\Delta R^2 = 41.1$

For Notes to Tables, see page 49.
Source: Compiled by the author.

In general, the present study did not find significant relationships between most of the indexes of health and city size or urbanized area growth rate. Neither bronchitis, emphysema, or asthma deaths, motor vehicle deaths, nor infant deaths were found to be significantly associated with either predictor, either before or after inclusion of test factors. Cirrhosis deaths appear to be significantly related to growth (not size), although this relationship does not emerge until three test factors are introduced (region, median age in the city, and percent black or Spanish origin in the city). In Table 4.1 one can see that size and growth alone account for only about 6 percent of the variance in cirrhosis deaths. Including the test factors increases the growth effect moderately ($beta_{ET}^2$ = .10), while leaving size unaffected—the principal difference lying between places which have lost population and those which have grown (rates are almost 50 percent higher in the latter than in the former: 17.6 per 10,000 vs. 11.6). Death rates from cirrhosis are higher in cities located in growing urbanized areas outside the South, characterized by relatively older populations and higher percentages of blacks and Spanish-Americans. The growth effect per se, while significant, is moderate ($beta_{ET}^2$ = 10.2); the effect of size and growth net of the test factors is only about 10 percent.

The pattern of relationships for suicides is similar to that observed for cirrhosis. In Table 4.2 one notes the absence of significant city-size effects; growth effects are weak but statistically significant. Introducing test factors slightly strengthens the relationship between growth and suicide rates ($beta_{ET}^2$ = .06). Again, main effects are minor relative to those of the test factors; while the full model accounts for a little more than half the variance in suicide rates, size and growth net of the test factors account for only about 11 percent. Significant test factors include the three noted previously for cirrhosis, as well as median adult schooling in the city (rates are higher in cities characterized by relatively better-educated populations).

With respect to public health, one may conclude that size effects do not exist for any of the five indicators; weak growth effects are observed for two (cirrhosis and suicides), particularly when test factors are introduced to strengthen the relationships. Inasmuch as both cirrhosis and suicides are hypothesized to reflect social disorganization, one may speculate that growing areas may be so characterized relative to other places; this is consistent with Weschler (1961). On the other hand, one cannot say whether growing areas tend to produce disorganizing experiences, or whether persons prone to suicide and alcoholism tend to migrate to such places.

CRIME

Measured crime rates tend to increase with city size, although problems with measuring and interpreting crime data are notorious. Many studies have noted a simple correlation between city population and crime rates per capita (e.g., Duncan 1951:764; Alonso 1973:197; Hoch 1972a:271-72; Hoch 1972b:323)—and that expenditures on police increase with city size, suggesting that "the large city experiences not only a greater relative amount of crime, but also pays proportionately more heavily for it" (Duncan 1951:764). There is some evidence that larger cities have somewhat higher rates for some categories of crimes even when differences in racial composition, age, income, education, crowding, and other related variables are taken into account. Hoch (1972a) found that among 56 cities of over 250,000 persons, city size remained significantly associated only with rape among violent crimes, once these other factors were controlled. A similar examination of crimes in 99 California cities found that city size remained significant for robbery and theft as well as rape (1972a:271-72), but the effects of population are considerably reduced once other factors were controlled. Hoch concludes that "it is likely there is some increase in overall crime costs with city size and density, for a given racial mix" (1972b:323)—but that the differences are principally explained by other factors associated with city size.

TABLE 4.3

Effects of City Population and Urbanized Area Rate of Growth, and Selected Test Factors, on City Murders and Homicides
(rates per 10,000 population)

PART I: Mean Values of Explanatory Factor Categories

Grand Mean = 9.90

Grand Standard Deviation = 6.76

Total Number of Cases = 77

Explanatory Factor	Number of Cases	Unadjusted Means	Means Adjusted For:	
			Explanatory Factors	Explanatory and Test Factors
POPULATION				
50,000–62,000	5	12.47	12.76	8.18
62,000–75,000	10	7.46	7.42	7.25
75,000–120,000	20	8.49	8.26	8.60
120,000–175,000	23	8.73	8.74	10.67
175,000–400,000	19	13.41	13.58	12.18
Association:		$eta^a = .34$	$beta_E{}^b = .36$	$beta_{ET}{}^c = .26$
Significance of F:[d]		$p_F = .002$	$p_F = .002$	$p_F = .044$
GROWTH RATE '60–'70				
"negative" (<10%)	21	9.57	10.18	10.58
moderate (10%–25%)	25	10.00	9.13	9.59

rapid (25% and above)

	eta	$beta_E$	$beta_{ET}$
	10.04	10.33	9.69
Association:	$eta^a = .03$	$beta_E{}^b = .08$	$beta_{ET}{}^c = .06$
Significance of F:[d]	$p_F = .999$	$p_F = .999$	$p_F = .999$
(100) · MULTIPLE R² =	—	12.0	63.0

31

PART II: Summary Statistics, Explanatory Factors

Expl. Factor	Measure of Association			Marginal Variance Added:[e]	
	$(100) \cdot eta^{2\,a}$	$(100) \cdot beta_E{}^{2\,b}$	$(100) \cdot beta_{ET}{}^{2\,c}$	Each expl. factor, net of other ΔR^2	Expl. factors, net of test factors ΔR^2
POPULATION GROWTH RATE	11.6	13.0	6.8	11.9	$\left.\begin{array}{c} \\ \end{array}\right\}$ 6.1
	0.1	0.6	0.4	0.4	

PART III: Summary Statistics, Test Factors

Test Factor	b^f	Significance $(p_{F_b})^g$
Region	3.83	.009
Metropolitan Consolidation	-6.92	.027
% black or Spanish-American	.27	.001

Marginal Variance Added, Test Factors net of Explanatory Factors[h] $\Delta R^2 = 51.0$

For Notes to Tables, see page 49.
Source: Compiled by the author.

61

TABLE 4.4

Effects of City Population and Urbanized Area Rate of Growth, and Selected Test Factors, on City Robberies and Burglaries
(rates per 10,000 population)

PART I: Mean Values of Explanatory Factor Categories
Grand Mean = 1651.0
Grand Standard Deviation = 638.4
Total Number of Cases = 77

Explanatory Factor	Number of Cases	Unadjusted Means	Means Adjusted For: Explanatory Factors	Explanatory and Test Factors
POPULATION				
50,000–62,000	5	1351.1	1287.6	972.0
62,000–75,000	10	1478.8	1436.6	1423.0
75,000–120,000	20	1584.1	1663.0	1618.0
120,000–175,000	23	1622.3	1579.6	1769.1
175,000–400,000	19	1925.4	1933.2	1841.3
Association:		$eta^a = .27$	$beta_E^b = .30$	$beta_{ET}^c = .35$
Significance of F:[d]		$p_F = .178$	$p_F = .035$	$p_F = .010$
GROWTH RATE '60–'70				
"negative" (< 10%)	21	1401.9	1375.9	1615.8
moderate (10%–25%)	25	1621.6	1611.2	1698.5

rapid (25% and above)
Association:
Significance of F:[d]
$(100) \cdot$ MULTIPLE $R^2 =$

	31	1843.3 $eta^a = .28$ $p_F = .029$	1869.3 $beta_E{}^b = .32$ $p_F = .005$ 16.7	1635.5 $beta_{ET}{}^c = .05$ $p_F = .999$ 48.9

PART II: Summary Statistics, Explanatory Factors

	Measure of Association			Marginal Variance Added:[e]	
				Each expl. factor, net of other	Expl. factors, net of test factors
Expl. Factor	$(100) \cdot eta^{2a}$	$(100) \cdot beta_E{}^{2b}$	$(100) \cdot beta_{ET}{}^{2c}$	ΔR^2	ΔR^2
POPULATION	7.3	9.0	12.3	8.9	} 11.8
GROWTH RATE	7.8	10.2	0.3	9.4	

PART III: Summary Statistics, Test Factors

Test Factor	b^f	Significance $(p_{F_b})^g$
Median adult schooling	265.4	.018
Metropolitan Consolidation	-1596.7	.001
% black or Spanish-American	20.2	.001

Marginal Variance Added, Test Factors net of Explanatory Factors[h] $\Delta R^2 = 32.2$

For Notes to Tables, see page 49.
Source: Compiled by the author.

Murders and Homicides

Table 4.3 summarizes the data for these two classes of serious crimes. There is no relationship between growth and per capita rates of murders and homicides; the effect of size per se is nonlinear. One notes in column 2 that rates are highest in both the smallest and largest places—although the relationship with size is generally weak overall (eta^2 = .12, $beta^2_E$ = .13). I can presently offer no explanation for this U-shaped curve. Introducing the test factors alters the shape of this curve, with rates being lowest in cities of under 75,000 and then increasing linearly thereafter. A difference of almost 60 percent separates those cities with the lowest rates from those with the highest when all factors one considered (7.6 per 10,000 in cities under 75,000; 12.2 in cities of 175,000-400,000; $beta_{ET}$ = .26)—although perhaps not too much should be made of such differences in light of the relatively low incidence of such crimes overall (fewer than one per thousand population on the average; the range over all the cities is from 0 to 3.3). The influence of the test factors on murder-homicide rates is considerably greater than that of growth and size; the marginal variance predicted by the latter net of the former is 51 percent, while that predicted by size and growth net of the three test factors is only 6.1 percent. Rates of homicide and murder are higher in cities outside the South, in cities characterized by a high percentage of blacks and Spanish-Americans, and in cities which are relatively "unconsolidated" (that is, are small relative to their surrounding urbanized population). This latter variable is of particular interest in this context; it suggests that crime rates within the city might be as much a function of total area population. This, in turn, might be one reason why city expenditures have been found to correlate more strongly with suburban population than with city population (Hawley 1951; Kasarda 1972). Alternatively, however, this finding might be due to the fact that in larger urban areas the boundary lines of the city have come to approximate the urbanized area core—which may be an area of relatively high crime rates.

Robberies and Burglaries

This second category of crimes exhibits a weak linear relationship with both size and growth; furthermore, the effects appear to be relatively independent of one another, with each contributing about half of the 17 percent of the variance accounted for by both together. The difference in rates between cities in the smallest and largest size categories is about 50 percent when growth is taken into account (1288 offences per 10,000 residents, vs. 1933; $beta_E$ = .30), while the differences between cities losing in population and those rapidly gaining is 36 percent controlling on size (1376 vs. 1869; $beta_E$ = .32). Three test factors proved to be important influences on robbery and burglary rates: lack of "metropolitan consolidation," percentage black or of Spanish origin in the city, and median adult education in the city were all found to be positively associated with crime rates. The effect of including these variables is to strengthen the original relationship between central-city population size and the robbery-burglary rate; the differential between the smallest and largest cities is close to 90 percent ($beta_{ET}$ = .35) when all factors are considered. The effects of growth, on the other hand, are reduced to nonsignificance.

It is perhaps noteworthy that median income did not enter significantly into the model; under the hypothesis that "opportunities" for crime are predictive of rates, the contrary would be expected. It should also be noted that there is no support for the hypothesis that the social disorganization possibly characteristic of rapidly growing areas is responsible for higher crime rates; under the full model (all factors included), growth itself no longer is a source of variation in these crimes against property, while size emerges as a stronger source of variation. About 49 percent of the variance can be accounted for by all factors; the test factors, net of size and growth, contribute about 32 percent, while the latter net of the former contribute only 12 percent.

TABLE 4.5

Effects of City Population and Urbanized Area Rate of Growth, and Selected Test Factors, on City Automobile Thefts
(rates per 10,000 population)

PART I: Mean Values of Explanatory Factor Categories
Grand Mean = 485.41
Grand Standard Deviation = 259.23
Total Number of Cases = 100

Explanatory Factor	Number of Cases	Unadjusted Means	Means Adjusted For: Explanatory Factors	Explanatory and Test Factors
POPULATION				
50,000–62,000	15	399.62	382.80	315.07
62,000–75,000	19	417.74	420.40	391.26
75,000–120,000	23	436.42	457.18	457.03
120,000–175,000	24	492.88	488.69	544.36
175,000–400,000	19	670.68	661.46	673.92
Association:		$eta^a = .37$	$beta_E{}^b = .36$	$beta_{ET}{}^c = .46$
Significance of F:d		$p_F = .007$	$p_F = .003$	$p_F = .001$
GROWTH RATE '60–'70				
"negative" (< 10%)	31	424.86	437.15	489.88
moderate (10%–25%)	36	526.63	524.60	559.05

rapid (25% and above)

		33		
Association:		497.32 $eta^a = .16$	487.99 $beta_E b = .14$	400.88 $beta_{ET}^c = .25$
Significance of F:d		$p_F = .264$	$p_F = .316$	$p_F = .039$
(100) · MULTIPLE R^2 =		—	15.3	35.9

PART II: Summary Statistics, Explanatory Factors

				Marginal Variance Added:[e]	
	Measure of Association			Each expl. factor, net of other	Expl. factors, net of test factors
Expl. Factor	$(100) \cdot eta^{2\,a}$	$(100) \cdot beta_E^{2\,b}$	$(100) \cdot beta_{ET}^{2\,c}$	ΔR^2	ΔR^2
POPULATION	13.7	13.0	21.2	12.7	} 22.2
GROWTH RATE	2.6	2.0	6.3	1.6	

PART III: Summary Statistics, Test Factors

Test Factor	b^f	Significance $(p_{F_b})^g$
City Density	- .03	
"Metropolitan Consolidation"	-697.28	

Marginal Variance Added, Test Factors net of Explanatory Factors[h] $\Delta R^2 = 20.6$

For Notes to Tables, see page 49.
Source: Compiled by the author.

Automobile Thefts

Automobile thefts exhibit a pattern similar to that of the previous category of crimes. Size appears to be significantly associated with the rate of car thefts independently of growth; the inclusion of test factors further strengthens the estimated relationship. The difference between the smallest and largest quintile of cities is about two-thirds when size alone is considered (40 per 10,000, vs. 671; *eta* = .37); the differential doubles when all factors are considered. Growth appears to exert a weak inverse U-shaped effect, with rates somewhat higher in moderately growing urbanized areas than in the other two categories; but the association is not statistically significant. Again, "consolidation" is a moderately strong predictor of the crime rate, as is, to a lesser extent, city density—the higher the density, the lower the rate of automobile thefts. This undoubtedly reflects the fact that city density is inversely correlated with automobile owner-ship,[2] providing lesser opportunity for this category of crime in denser places.

NOTES

1. He examined adult and infant mortality, suicide, tuberculosis, venereal disease, juvenile delinquency, admission to mental hospitals and prisons, and illegitimacy.

2. The simple correlation between "owns two or more cars" and city density is − .26; between "uses public transportation and density the correlation is   .21.

5

SIZE, GROWTH, AND THE PUBLIC SECTOR

The public sector refers to the provision of goods and services to citizens by governmental entities of all types. Among the principal services typically provided by munici-pal-level government are police and fire protection, schools, parks and recreation, public works, streets and highways, and water sanitation. Studies have typically focused on city government, although some have looked additionally at special service districts or county government.

EARLIER STUDIES

The earliest studies of municipal services assumed that per resident costs for any service would tend to decline with increasing city size, due to economics of scale, until some optimum city size were reached; thereafter, costs would once again increase. The existence of a U-shaped curve has been readily established for most city services. The initial empirical studies[1] were done in England, and found per capita costs for many urban services to be lowest in cities from about 100,000 to 250,000 residents (for example, Baker 1910; London County Council 1915); these findings were readily

replicated in later studies of British and U.S. municipalities (Oxford District, 1938; Phillips 1942; Lomax 1943),
although some studies (e.g., Ogburn 1937) placed the optimal
size somewhat lower and found cities of 50,000–100,000 to be
optimal with respect to costs. A principal source of rising
costs in the largest cities was found to be the police function;
Walker (1930) established that an increasing proportion of
city budgets went to pay for police as cities grew in size. On
the other hand, Duncan (1951), reviewing other studies as
well as municipal finance data for U.S. cities during the
forties, concluded that for 14 categories of expenditure, "the
larger cities spend more for highways, sanitation, public welfare, correction, schools, etc., than small" (1951:766); however, he cautioned against interpreting these results in terms
of municipal efficiency, since "these data reflect the separ-
ately varying factors of unit costs, amount, and quality of
sercices" (Ibid.). Larger cities may have greater problems
than smaller ones (hence higher per capita expenditures may
not reflect inefficiency); furthermore, "the higher levels of
expenditures for schools, libraries, and education apparently
reflect greater amounts and/or qualities of these services"
(Ibid.).

More recent studies have employed multivariate techniques to determine whether quality and output vary systematically with city size, while looking for other correlates of
size which might account for the previously noted relationships between size and per capita service costs.[2] Thus, for
example, a study conducted for the Advisory Commission on
Intergovernmental Relations looked at medium-sized cities
within various states, thereby standardizing for differences
between states in local financing and types of services provided by municipalities (ACIR 1968). This study employed
regression analyses for such services as police and fire protection, highways, sewage and sanitation, parks and recreation,
and general government for cities of 25,000 to 250,000 in
Ohio, Texas, and New Jersey. No relationship between per
capita and population was found, leading the authors to conclude that for these services in medium-sized cities "population by itself does not generally result in any major economies or diseconomies of scale" (ACIR 1968:47). On the

other hand, in comparison with larger cities (over 250,000 persons), some functions did appear to be associated with higher per capita costs in some states; for example, Ohio municipalities larger than 471,000 tended to spend progressively more on police, sanitation, and parks and recreation, while cities over 290,000 spent more on fire (Ibid.). Similar patterns were observed in the other states, although for different services; "at least for certain functions in certain states, the larger cities do produce diseconomies of scale" (Ibid.:50). Another method of standardizing for differences in the local provision of services has been to look at total expenditures aggregated by county; it is argued that such an approach eliminates differences that might be due to variations in the distribution of governmental units (Schmandt and Stephens 1963). Studies based on the 1957 census of governments—which provided such county aggregates—found the highest per capita expenditures on commonly shared functions to be in the smallest and largest counties (Shapiro 1963:108; Schmandt and Stephens 1963:400-1); this was found to be particularly true of current (as opposed to capital) expenditures. The lowest expenditures were found to lie in counties containing between 25,000 and 100,000 persons. Schmandt and Stephens concluded that "the data suggest that both the very large and the very small counties suffer from diseconomies of scale" (1963:400–401).

The same writers question, however, that the explanation lies entirely with economies of scale. Several studies have suggested that the principal determinant of local spending is the ability to spend, as measured by such indexes as median income, assessed property value, and intergovernmental revenues. One study by Scott and Feder (1957) of some 200 California cities over 25,000 in population employed a curvilinear regression analysis[3] to predict gross municipal spending on the basis of a number of variables; while five variables were significant in accounting for 70 percent of the variance (population, per capita retail sales, crowding, rate of growth, and per capita property value), one of these—per capita property value—itself accounted for four-fifths of the explained variance. The Scott and Feder study suggested that availability of resources may in large part explain differences in

spending patterns. A number of studies have found that
median family income is positively related to city size (these
are reviewed below); insofar as size is related to per capita
expenditures on such services as fire and police protection, it
is argued that larger cities have more wealth to protect and
are willing to spend more on these major services as a result
(see Schmandt and Stephens 1963:403–405).

The Scott and Feder study concluded that population
itself is of secondary importance in accounting for per capita
expenditures on the services studied, once measures of wealth
and fiscal capacity are taken into account. Their conclusions
must be qualified, however, in that they did not separate capital from current operating expenditures, and in that their
analysis included cities that lay within larger metropolitan
regions (principally Los Angeles) as well as isolated or relatively "independent" cities.[4] This latter limitation bears
special emphasis, for it is common to many of the studies
reviewed below. While no city is truly "independent" ecolog-
ically or economically, cities can be classified according to
the degree to which they are relatively self-contained—that is,
are not suburbs and/or contiguous to other cities. Subur-
ban/contiguous cities may have unique patterns of service
costs. On the one hand, they may provide services for commuting residents of neighboring municipalities that comprise
the larger metropolitan region, thereby inflating local costs;
on the other hand, they often share in service costs through
special service district arrangements or with county governmental bodies. To lump relatively self-contained cities
together with cities that are merely political subdivisions of
large metropolitan areas is to invite spurious findings.

A study which attempted to take such considerations
into account was conducted by Brazer for the National
Bureau of Economic Research (Brazer 1959). In his principal
analysis, Brazer examined 1951 expenditures in 462 incorporated places with populations over 25,000, on a number of
common functions (police, fire, highways, recreation, sanitation, and general control) as well as total spending. Capital
expenditures were, in general, excluded from the analysis. A linear multiple regression analysis was employed,
in which expenditures were predicted by population,

density, rate of population increase, median family income, per capita intergovernmental revenue, and percent of population employed in manufacturing, trade, and services. For all of the cities, these six variables accounted for almost three-fifths of the variance in total expenditures, although individual services varied widely in the degree to which they were predicted. Of the six independent variables, only population density, median family income, and per capita intergovernmental revenue proved to be consistently important; population itself was weakly associated with only a single service expenditure (police) once the other variables were simultaneously considered. One possible interpretation is that Brazer's use of linear model to describe the relationship between population size and per capita costs proved insensitive to the actual relationship, which numerous studies have found to be curvilinear. Brazer does not, however, provide data pertinent to this concern.

Another possible explanation, considered by Brazer, is the divergence between the politically incorporated city and urban area (the difficulty mentioned above)—the fact that the census population of cities often diverges from the population actually receiving services (Brazer 1959:28).[5] Hawley, in an earlier (1951) study of cities over 100,000 people,[6] had found that per capita city expenditures were more strongly associated with the size of the population outside the city boundaries than with the population inside, particularly when the former is expressed as a proportion of the total population. Hawley concluded that city residents are paying for services consumed by their satellite populations; this in turn, indicated the need for a single planning, taxing, and jurisdictional unit. Numerous other studies have echoed this finding (Kee 1967; Margolis 1957; Vincent 1968; Finkler 1972; Kasarda 1972; Shapiro 1963); according to one, "the 'balkanization' of many metropolitan areas has added to the problem [of high level service requirements] as the central cities are faced with the need to provide services to nontax-paying commuters" (Shapiro 1963:178). Brazer explained this hypothesis in a substudy of per capita expenditures of 40 larger cities (over 250,000) and their overlying unit of government. In addition to the independent variables employed in his larger multiple regression analysis of 462 cities, Brazer included three new ones: the proportion of the population in public schools, per capita state expenditures on welfare in the city, and the ratio of city population to that of its surrounding SMSA. The latter variable was intended to test the "commutation" hypothesis. Brazer was able to predict about three-quarters of the variance in total general operating expenditures, although the range of predictability of individual services varied widely (Brazer 1959:4-55). He found that population density, per capita intergovernmental revenue, and the ratio of city to metropolitan area population were the strongest and most consistent predictors of city expenditures; neither population level nor rate of growth was significantly associated with any of the various expenditure categories once the other variables were taken into account. The "commutation" variable was strongly associated with both total general operating expenses and such common function expenditures as police and fire.

The difficulty with treating commutation exclusively as a cost to municipal services is that nonresidents may bring benefits as well. In addition to such noneconomic benefits as support for local cultural activities, commuters increase local income through their personal expenditures within the city: Their purchases of goods may contribute to municipal revenues in states such as California where cities receive a portion of the retail sales tax for general revenue purposes, and by their support of the commercial sector they may contribute to heightened commercial property values and hence greater revenues to the city from property taxes. Thus, it is not clear that commuters exploit the central city, on the balance; and some studies suggest that when all factors are taken into account, commutation may be a net benefit (Kee 1967; see especially Baum 1971).[7]

In looking at total expenditures on public education, Hirsch found that a district's financial ability (as indexed by the average assessed value of property per pupil attending) was the most important single determinant of expenditures; the total number of pupils (which might be taken as analogous to total population in terms of demand for services) was not a significant source of variation. Hirsch concludes that "perhaps the most important single finding is the absence of significant economies of scale in the St. Louis City-County area" (Hirsch 1960:36); elsewhere he notes that in general, "efficiency considerations, thus, do not appear to warrant across-the-board consolidation of metropolitan area governments" (Hirsch 1959:240). With the exception of water and sewage, where economies of scale may obtain (Ibid.; but see also Hoch 1972:260–63), "economic efficiency may be highest in medium-sized communities of 50,000–100,000 residents" (ibid.).

The relationship between city size and public expenditures is by no means as clear-cut as earlier writers assumed. Although a single examination of the relationship generally produces a U-shaped curve, once other factors are considered the importance of population becomes unclear. Principal among these are the financial ability to provide high levels of services (indexed by average property value, median income, or the level of intergovernmental revenues), density, the size of the city relative to its surrounding urban area, and the quality of service provided. Thus, many of the most recent writers have concluded that population itself is generally unrelated to the cost of providing city services, either across the entire range of city sizes (Brazer 1959:66, Bollens and Schmandt 1965:365; Scott and Feder 1957:31) or at least for small- and medium-sized cities (ACIR 1968:52; Finkler 1972:20). On the other hand, these conclusions appear to be based on a limited number of empirical studies, the two principal ones (Brazer 1959; Scott and Feder 1957) having methodological shortcomings detailed previously which make interpretation of their results difficult. A more recent study concludes that population remains important, although the other variables previously mentioned must also be taken into account. Baum (1971), employing 1960 data for cities in The Netherlands, estimated the effect of city size on what he termed "per capita disposable income," the latter being the difference between per capita gross income (itself a function of such variables as city size and growth rate, percentage of city labor force that is in-commuting, density, and percentage of school-age population) and per capita cost of public services (a function of size, percentage in-commuting, percentage school age, and percentage senior citizens). Baum concludes that the optimal size for Dutch cities is about one-half million in relation to per capita disposable income; actual estimates range from 482,000 persons (as a function of size alone) to 522,000 (as a function of size, controlling on growth and commutation) (Baum 1971:61). He also notes that such variables as commutation, percentage of senior and school-age population, and density are more important than either size or growth in explaining per capita costs, gross income, and disposable income (1971:57-60). Baum concludes that "the inclusion of private income in the estimating procedure raises the optimal city size considerably beyond the levels usually found in the previous analyses. It argues that many of the cities of the size we witness today may not only be tolerable, but also are relatively efficient" (1971:64). His conclusions, however, must be qualified (as he indeed notes) to the extent that income and costs are adequate measures of the value of private and public goods and services. For example, to the extent that cost-of-living or environmental costs increase with city size, Baum's measures of per capita disposable income may overestimate the actual value of "real" income in larger cities, in terms of the quantity and especially quality of goods and services that income will purchase (for another difficulty with Baum's conclusions, see footnote 7).

PRESENT STUDY

It is difficult to compare cities with respect to expenditures on public services, due to wide variations in the sorts of services provided. The same difficulty affects comparisons of revenues, either in the form of property tax rates or amounts per capita. Because of such considerations, comparisons are limited to three expenditure items common to all cities: police and fire protection, and common function personnel. The latter category includes those functions performed by most cities, including police and fire protection, highways, wastewater and sanitation, parks and recreation, and water supply. Even such comparisons must be qualified, however, because of possible differences in quality of services between places.

Fire Protection

In Table 5.1 one can note that while there is no relationship between city size and per capita expenditures on fire protection, there is a very weak relationship with urbanized area growth rate, although this relationship does not become statistically significant until the associated effects of two test factors are taken into account ("metropolitan consolidation" and median income). Urbanized areas that have lost population during the period 1960–70 have somewhat higher expenditures per capita on this service—the difference between this category and the two growth categories being about 16 percent ($beta_{ET}^2$ equals .08). The effects of growth, however, are minor relative to the effects of median family income in the city, and "consolidation." Cities which are large relative to their surrounding urbanized areas spend relatively less on fire protection, as do cities with lower median incomes. A decrease of one thousand dollars on the latter variable is associated with a decrease of about one and three-quarters dollars per person on fire protection. While the inclusion of all factors enables one to account for almost two-fifths of the variance in this governmental expenditure, size and growth together account for only 6.3 percent. It may be concluded that size effects per se are nonexistent, and growth effects are negligible, for this service.

Police

The pattern with respect to expenditures on police is similar to that for fire protection (Table 5.2). Although I have previously noted the higher rates for certain categories of crime in larger cities, police expenditures do not appear to be significantly higher in such places. The difference between the smallest and largest categories of cities is about one-eighth, with this difference increasing somewhat when urban-

TABLE 5.1

Effects of City Population and Urbanized Area Rate of Growth, and Selected Test Factors, on City Per Capita Expenditures on Fire Protection ($)

PART I: Mean Values of Explanatory Factor Categories

Grand Mean = 16.49

Grand Standard Deviation = 5.02

Total Number of Cases = 93

Explanatory Factor	Number of Cases	Unadjusted Means	Means Adjusted For:	
			Explanatory Factors	Explanatory and Test Factors
POPULATION				
50,000–80,000	13	16.00	16.61	16.32
80,000–125,000	18	16.14	16.28	16.36
125,000–175,000	21	15.94	15.56	15.30
175,000–275,000	23	17.68	17.45	17.85
275,000–400,000	18	16.32	16.46	16.39
Association:		$eta^a = .14$	$beta_E{}^b = .13$	$beta_{ET}{}^c = .18$
Significance of F:[d]		$p_F = .999$	$p_F = .999$	$p_F = .999$
GROWTH RATE '60–'70				
"negative" (< 10%)	29	16.10	16.49	18.53
moderate (10%–25%)	32	14.92	15.18	15.48

rapid (25% and above)
Association:
Significance of F:[d]
$(100) \cdot$ MULTIPLE $R^2 =$ 32

17.87	17.81	15.65
$eta^a = .22$	$beta_E{}^b = .22$	$beta_{ET}{}^c = .28$
$p_F = .116$	$p_F = .054$	$p_F = .020$
—	6.3	39.8

PART II: Summary Statistics, Explanatory Factors

	Measure of Association			Marginal Variance Added:[e]	
				Each expl. factor, net of other	Expl. factors, net of test factors
Expl. Factor	$(100) \cdot eta^2{}^a$	$(100) \cdot beta_E{}^2{}^b$	$(100) \cdot beta_{ET}{}^2{}^c$	ΔR^2	ΔR^2
POPULATION	2.0	1.7	3.2	1.5	} 7.5
GROWTH RATE	4.8	4.8	7.8	4.3	

PART III: Summary Statistics, Test Factors

Test Factor	b^f	Significance $(p_{Fb})^g$
"Metropolitan Consolidation"	13.36	.001
Median Income ($000)	1.73	.001

Marginal Variance Added, Test Factors net of Explanatory Factors[h] $\Delta R^2 = 33.5$

For Notes to Tables, see page 49.
Source: Compiled by the author.

TABLE 5.2

Effects of City Population and Urbanized Area Rate of Growth, and Selected Test Factors, on City Per Capita Expenditures on Police ($)

PART I: Mean Values of Explanatory Factor Categories

Grand Mean = 18.06
Grand Standard Deviation = 6.17
Total Number of Cases = 89

Explanatory Factor	Number of Cases	Unadjusted Means	Means Adjusted For: Explanatory Factors	Means Adjusted For: Explanatory and Test Factors
POPULATION				
50,000–62,000	13	17.57	17.85	16.72
62,000–75,000	16	16.97	16.98	17.31
75,000–120,000	20	17.05	17.63	17.35
120,000–175,000	22	18.51	17.91	18.61
175,000–400,000	18	19.95	19.82	19.81
Association:		$eta^a = .18$	$beta_E{}^b = .15$	$beta_{ET}{}^c = .18$
Significance of F:d		$p_F = .999$	$p_F = .322$	$p_F = .226$
GROWTH RATE '60–'70				
"negative" (< 10%)	25	15.00	15.11	18.31
moderate (10%–25%)	32	18.25	18.15	18.57

rapid (25% and above)

	32		
Association:	$eta^a = .34$	$beta_E{}^b = .33$	$beta_{ET}{}^c = .09$
	20.27	20.27	17.35
Significance of F:d	$p_F = .005$	$p_F = .001$	$p_F = .999$
$(100) \cdot$ MULTIPLE $R^2 =$	—	14.0	62.3

PART II: Summary Statistics, Explanatory Factors

Expl. Factor	Measure of Association			Marginal Variance Added:^{e}	
	$(100) \cdot eta^{2a}$	$(100) \cdot beta_E{}^{2b}$	$(100) \cdot beta_{ET}{}^{2c}$	Each expl. factor, net of other ΔR^2	Expl. factors, net of test factors ΔR^2
POPULATION	3.2	2.3	3.2	2.4	$\left.\begin{array}{c} \\ \\ \end{array}\right\}$ 4.8
GROWTH RATE	11.6	10.9	0.8	10.8	

PART III: Summary Statistics, Test Factors

Test Factor	b^f	Significance $(p_{F_b})^g$
"Metropolitan Consolidation"	-19.75	.001
Median Family Income ($000)	2.28	.001

Marginal Variance Added, Test Factors net of Explanatory Factors^h ΔR^2: = 48.3

For Notes to Tables, see page 49.
Source: Compiled by the author.

ized area growth rate and the two test factors are considered; but the pattern of differences is not statistically significant.

With respect to growth, urbanized areas that have lost population have lower police expenditures than those which have not, and expenditures are highest in the fastest-growing areas. The difference between "negative" growth and rapid growth areas is more than one-third (approximately $15 vs. $20 per capita), with a difference between moderate and rapid growth of about 10 percent. These differences are apparently due to the associated effects of median income in the city and "consolidation," however; when the two test factors are included, the effects of urbanized area growth rate are eliminated. This is consistent with the findings of other studies, which have reported that city expenditures on such services as police are largely a function of local wealth (Scott and Feder 1957; Schmandt and Stephens 1963:403–5, Brazer 1959) and the degree to which city residents must subsidize the costs associated with surrounding areas (Hawley 1951; Shapiro 1963; Kasarda 1972; Brazer 1959). The effect of these two variables is, apparently, substantial. For example, a thousand dollar increase in city median family income is associated with a $2.28 increase in expenditures. All factors together account for over three-fifths of the variance in this expenditure; the marginal variance added by explanatory factors net of the test factors is estimated at only about 5 percent, while the two test factors net of the explanatory factors account for almost 50 percent.

Common City Functions: Numbers of Personnel and Total Costs

Tables 5.3 and 5.4 present the relationship between size and growth and both the numbers and costs of employees in those functions performed by most cities. The number of such personnel exhibits the U-shaped curve found in earlier studies. With respect to population size, the cities in the middle quintile (population of 75,000–120,000) have about 17 percent fewer common function employees than those in the smallest category and about 8 percent fewer than those in the larger (unadjusted means; see Table 5.2, column 2, Part I). These differences, however, cease to be statistically significant when the conjoint effects of the test factors—region and "consolidation"—are considered. The same is true with regard to urbanized area population growth rate: while the number of personnel is the lowest in moderately growing places, the difference is not significant when test factors are included. The two test factors net of the explanatory factors account for about 38 percent of the total variance; all factors together account for 50 percent, with the marginal variance added by explanatory factors net of the test factors estimated at only about 4 percent. Again, the absence of "consolidation" proves to be strongly associated with common function personnel, per capita. It also appears that the number of employees per capita is considerably lower outside the South—approximately six per thousand residents.

Differences in payroll costs associated with these personnel differentials are presented in Table 5.4. The same pattern emerges as in the previous table: expenditures are lower on the average in those cities in the middle quintile (75,000–120,000) and in those cities located in moderately growing urbanized areas. The size effect is more pronounced when growth is considered, and still more so when the single test factor is included—although the pattern is not statistically significant at the .05 level (p equals .06). Payroll expenditures per capita in cities in the middle category are about 12 percent lower than in those in the smallest category. The effects of urbanized area growth are more pronounced. Payroll expenditures per person are highest in cities located in those areas experiencing rapid growth ($beta_E^2$ equals .14), the difference between moderately growing areas and rapidly growing ones amounting to almost 30 percent when the effect of size is simultaneously considered. When "consolidation" is included, this difference is reduced to about 18 percent ($beta_{ET}^2$ equals .07), but remains statistically significant. Size, growth, and "consolidation" account for almost two-fifths of the variance in common function payroll expenditures per resident; the marginal variance added by the two explanatory factors net of the test factor is only about 12 percent, while that of the latter net of the former is close to 40 percent.

TABLE 5.3

Effects of City Population and Urbanized Area Rate of Growth, and Selected Test Factors, on City Common Function Personnel (numbers of personnel per 10,000 population)

PART I: Mean Values of Explanatory Factor Categories
Grand Mean = 88.02
Grand Standard Deviation = 21.66
Total Number of Cases = 97

Explanatory Factor	Number of Cases	Unadjusted Means	Means Adjusted For: Explanatory Factors	Explanatory and Test Factors
POPULATION				
50,000–62,000	15	97.24	101.08	91.81
62,000–75,000	18	88.00	88.93	87.73
75,000–120,000	22	83.30	80.77	81.94
120,000–175,000	24	85.22	84.00	89.93
175,000–400,000	18	89.87	90.45	90.03
Association:		$eta^a = .21$	$beta_E^b = .31$	$beta_{ET}^c = .16$
Significance of F:d		$p_F = .372$	$p_F = .008$	$p_F = .391$
GROWTH RATE '60–'70				
"negative" (< 10%)	31	86.99	88.66	92.13
moderate (10%–25%)	35	83.63	80.49	83.20

rapid (25% and above)
Association:
Significance of F:[d]

	31	94.01	95.87	89.36
		$eta^a = .20$	$beta_E{}^b = .29$	$beta_{ET}{}^c = .18$
		$p_F = .142$	$p_F = .002$	$p_F = .094$

$(100) \cdot$ MULTIPLE $R^2 =$ — 12.2 50.0

PART II: Summary Statistics, Explanatory Factors

	Measure of Association			Marginal Variance Added:[e]	
				Each expl. factor, net of other	Expl. factors, net of test factors
Expl. Factor	$(100) \cdot eta^2{}^a$	$(100) \cdot beta_E{}^{2\,b}$	$(100) \cdot beta_{ET}{}^{2\,c}$	ΔR^2	ΔR^2
POPULATION	4.4	9.6	2.6	8.2	} 3.6
GROWTH RATE	4.0	8.4	3.2	7.8	

PART III: Summary Statistics, Test Factors

Test Factor	b^f	Significance $(p_{F_b})^g$
Region	-55.16	.001
"Metropolitan Consolidation"	-19.65	.001

Marginal Variance Added, Test Factors net of Explanatory Factors[h] $\Delta R^2 = 37.8$

For Notes to Tables, see page 49.   *Source:* Compiled by the author.

TABLE 5.4

Effects of City Population and Urbanized Area Rate of Growth, and Selected Test Factors, on City Payroll Per Capita
($)

PART I: Mean Values of Explanatory Factor Categories

Grand Mean = 4.86
Grand Standard Deviation = 1.33
Total Number of Cases = 97

Explanatory Factor	Number of Cases	Unadjusted Means	Means Adjusted For:	
			Explanatory Factors	Explanatory and Test Factors
POPULATION				
50,000–62,000	15	5.02	5.29	4.99
62,000–75,000	18	4.52	4.63	4.46
75,000–120,000	22	4.57	4.45	4.47
120,000–175,000	24	4.95	4.81	5.09
175,000–400,000	18	5.29	5.30	5.31
Association:		$eta^a = .21$	$beta_E{}^b = .25$	$beta_{ET}{}^c = .26$
Significance of F:d		$p_F = .355$	$p_F = .074$	$p_F = .060$
GROWTH RATE '60–'70				
"negative" (< 10%)	31	4.52	4.64	4.89
moderate (10%–25%)	35	4.51	4.37	4.46

rapid (25% and above)

		5.59	5.63	5.28
Association:		$eta^a = .38$	$beta_E{}^b = .41$	$beta_{ET}{}^c = .26$
Significance of F:d		$p_F = .001$	$p_F = .001$	$p_F = .018$
$(100) \cdot$ MULTIPLE $R^2 =$	31	—	20.1	39.4

PART II: Summary Statistics, Explanatory Factors

	Measure of Association			Marginal Variance Added:[e]	
				Each expl. factor, net of other	Expl. factors, net of test factors
Expl. Factor	$(100) \cdot eta^{2a}$	$(100) \cdot beta_E{}^{2b}$	$(100) \cdot beta_{ET}{}^{2c}$	ΔR^2	ΔR^2
POPULATION	4.4	6.3	6.8	5.7	⎫
GROWTH RATE	14.4	16.8	6.8	15.7	⎬ 11.9

PART III: Summary Statistics, Test Factors

Test Factor	b^f	Significance $(p_{F_b})^g$
"Metropolitan Consolidation"	-3.13	.001

Marginal Variance Added, Test Factors net of Explanatory Factors[h] $\Delta R^2 = 19.3$

For Notes to Tables, see page 49.
Source: Compiled by the author.

One may conclude that despite the lack of significant relationship between urbanized area growth rate and the number of common function city personnel per capita, payroll costs are lowest in those areas growing at a moderate decennial rate of 10-25 percent. This suggests that the cost associated with each employee rises significantly as a function of growth, although the number of employees per resident does not (although, as noted, there is a weak, if nonsignificant, substantive relationship). Size itself shows a weak and statistically nonsignificant U-shaped pattern with respect to both the number of employees and payroll costs per capita. Again, the test factors prove to be stronger and more consistent predictors of costs than either size or growth. Consistent with the studies cited previously, "metropolitan consolidation" is a consistent predictor of public sector costs and personnel: cities surrounded by large urbanized areas outside the city limits are apparently subsidizing some of the expenses incurred by these populations. It should also be noted that median family income is associated with expenditures on fire and police protection, although not with common function personnel or payroll. This is consistent with the hypothesis that expenditures of this particular type are higher in those places with greater wealth to protect.

A NOTE ON THE NONMONETARY
EFFECTS OF SIZE AND GROWTH
ON THE PUBLIC SECTOR

Even if one concludes that population ceases to be statistically important once other influences are considered, it seems incorrect to thereby conclude that population is substantively unimportant as well. If, for example, greater political fragmentation is generally associated with higher population levels and is itself largely responsible for rising costs in larger cities, what does this imply for the effects of growth? Fragmentation can, of course, be mitigated to some extent by local policy. Cities may annex their surrounding communities so as to secure taxes from those commuters who use city services. But such actions require an aggressive approach to municipal government; furthermore, they entail major costs as well—costs that are hard to quantify and measure.

Principal among more "qualitative" costs are those associated with increasing bureaucratization of government. "Very large governments . . . are too far removed from the people, and often prove unresponsive to their needs and desires. People tend to lose interest, and their attitudes . . . can become negative" (Hirsch 1960:40; see also Task Force on Local Government Reform 1974:26-30). Growth, as Finkler notes, "presents problems not only in representation, but in administrative complexity and bureaucracy" (1972:23). The relationship between city size and political participation has all but been ignored in the literature on growth impacts, in part because of difficulties in conceptualizing and operationalizing the problem. Nonetheless, it seems clear that under an elective form of government, the larger the electorate, the lesser the direct contact between individuals and their political representatives, and the higher the costs of running (and winning) elections. The ideal of town meeting democracy—which, as has been noted, dates back to Plato and Aristotle in Western culture—can be realized only in the smallest of cities. Perhaps such costs can also be offset by adequate planning or innovative approaches to governmental organization, but little evidence exists historically for such precedents.

NOTES

1. For a survey of early studies and their findings, see Baum 1971.

2. While recent studies have attempted to correct for spurious relationships by employing curvilinear models and multivariate methods, those localities directly concerned with controlling growth have been largely ignorant of these studies, basing their own conclusions on a combination of purely local projections and simple comparisons between per capita costs and city size for all cities. The latter information is generally based on U.S. census figures and often does not attempt to standardize for service delivery (that is, the fact that in larger metropolitan areas, municipalities may share in the costs of certain area-wide services, or that there are statewide differences in those services which are allocated to cities). See, for example, the study conducted for the Pikes Peak Area Council of Governments (Bradley 1973); the Task

Force on Local Givernment Reform (1974:10-14); or the Sierra Club
study of San Diego (1973:14-15). Recent studies which are based on
purely local projections—and which come to opposite conclusions—include the Levy and Arnold (1972) study of Milpitas, California and the
Gruen and Gruen (1972) study of Livermore-Pleasanton, California.

3. A curvilinear analysis is sensitive to the U-shape of the per
capita expenditures curve.

4. Scott and Feder found that small towns (resort areas or towns
serving large geographic hinterlands) had unusually high capital out-
lays; furthermore, many such cities tended to provide services for populations residing outside the city limits. They also tended not to share
service costs with other municipalities or rely on county services or
special service districts. Thus, the governmental costs in small towns
may have been overstated relative to those of cities within the Los
Angeles metropolitan area, many of which "represent thin slices carved
from the large metropolitan community of which they are a part"
(Scott and Feder 1957:27).

5. Separate analyses of cities in Ohio, Massachusetts, and California were conducted to control for differences in the allocation of
functional responsibilities between state and city governments. These
studies found that "rate of growth, employment, and intergovernmental
revenues are most important in explaining variation in expenditures
among California cities; in Massachusetts and Ohio, population size,
density, and median income, the other three variables, play similar roles"
(Brazer 1959:47). The importance of population in Massachusetts and
Ohio is attributed in large part to the skewed distribution of city size
in these states, producing spurious results. The importance of growth
rate in California is attributed to the rapid rate of growth of that state
during the period 1940-1950; the consistent negative association between growth rate and per capita expenditures is hypothesized as resulting from a lag between expanded service requirements and the provision of those services.

6. Hawley examined 76 cities of 100,000 or more persons and
their metropolitan districts, excluding cities which lay within other
metropolitan districts.

7. Baum concludes that "a 10 percent increase in commutation is
associated with a 1.13 percent to 1.26 percent increase in per capita
disposable income [gross income less public costs]. Hence, this result
also supports the conclusion that there is a positive net benefit associated with a rise in commutation. It must be recognized, however,
that this conclusion is valid only to the extent that a city's resident
labor force—that is, its local labor force—is fully employed and that
new job opportunities exist for a foreign labor force. Otherwise, foreign

workers would displace local workers, causing the level of unemployment among local workers to rise and the city's gross income to fall"
(Baum 1971:58). This restrictive assumption, on which Baum's analytic
model is based, would appear to seriously question the generalizability
of his conclusions. It is highly unlikely in the long run that a city can
guarantee full employment among its resident population while creating new jobs to attract nonresident workers; some portion of those
workers will settle in the city itself, increasing the demand for services
and contributing to local unemployment.

6

OTHER SIZE AND
GROWTH EFFECTS

There are a number of other consequences of growth and size that were not considered in the study. Here I briefly review other findings pertinent to such possible effects—those concerned with the physical environment, and those concerned with popular attitudes toward one's community.

THE PHYSICAL ENVIRONMENT

Larger cities tend to be denser, more congested with traffic, and, as a consequence, suffer higher air and water pollution than smaller cities. Duncan noted almost 25 years ago that increasing size meant that it takes longer to get to work, with the automobile and eventually mass transit necessary for travel within larger places; he found that families in cities of over 100,000 persons spent four times as much for nonautomotive transportation as those in smaller cities (1951:761-62). Duncan concluded that "the unequivocal indication is that the advantages of time, expenditure, and convenience all lie with the moderate or small city" (Ibid.). Other studies have since echoed this conclusion (for example, Neutze 1965:43-60). One study found that the median time spent by family heads in daily work trips increased from an average of 17 minutes in outlying nonmetropolitan areas to almost an hour in the central cities of the 12 largest SMSAs (Morgan, Sirageldin, and Baerwaldt 1966:80; see also Hoch 1972a:243, 269-70). More traffic also means higher noise levels in larger cities (Hoch 1972a:267-68; Dickerson, et al. 1970; Klein, et al. 1971:204; Bolt, Beranek and Newman, Inc., 1970; Santa Barbara Planning Task Force 1976:87-80; U.S. Environmental Protection Agency 1971:2-12); noise has deleterious effects on mental and physical health (see, for example, Berry, et al. 1974). Traffic congestion is also associated with higher per capita death rates from automobile accidents in larger cities (Duncan 1951:764-65). Because of higher traffic congestion and greater industrial concentration, larger cities also experience increasing levels of air pollution—particularly gaseous pollutants produced by vehicular emissions (reactive hydrocarbons, nitrogen oxides, and carbon monoxide), although pollution from stationary sources increases as well—both gaseous (those previously enumerated, along with ozone and sulfur oxides) and particulate (for a summary of studies detailing these conclusions, see Hoch 1972a:247-57). It appears, however, that some types of pollution will be substantially reduced in cities of all sizes, if the Federal Clean Air Act of 1970 is rigorously enforced, which at the present writing (1978) seems doubtful (Santa Barbara Planning Task Force 1976:72-87; Nordsieck, 1977). Other types of pollution—besides noise and air quality—also afflict larger cities; for example, liquid waste disposal problems become more severe, and despite engineering data that suggest substantial economies of scale in waste disposal, the experience is that the largest cities experience both diseconomies in disposal costs and pollution problems as well (see Hoch 1972a:260-63). Solid waste disposal also increasingly becomes a problem (Ibid.:266).

   In addition to congestion and pollution problems, there is also some evidence that larger cities significantly affect the climate of their environs: surface wind speed is reduced (due to the presence of buildings), a "heat island" is created with temperature differentials as high as 20° F. in the evenings, and precipitation may rise by as much as 10 percent. These factors together may further exacerbate pollution problems, although whether the effects on the balance are desirable or not remains unclear (see Hoch 1972a:257–58 for a summary of studies).

With respect to other aspects of the physical environment, there is some evidence that larger cities have older, more dilapidated, and more crowded housing (Hadden and Borgatta 1965:108, 112). Larger cities also have less park space per capita than smaller cities, although the amount and variety of facilities (and corresponding costs) may be higher. Duncan concludes that "the optimum population for parks . . . is clearly the middle-size range of cities" in terms of such criteria as variety of facilities, per capita expenditures for operation and maintenance, and park space per resident (1951:769). As cities grow, undeveloped urban land becomes increasingly scarce and hence costly; park acquisition and development costs accordingly tend to rise.

ATTITUDES TOWARD CITY LIFE

The opinions of a city's residents, according to the assumption of a democratic society, are supposed to be a determinant of its public policies. To the extent that a city's growth pattern is determined by public policy—in the form of incentives and land-use measures that encourage or restrict growth—one may ascertain the degree to which such policies reflect public opinion. One cost or benefit of a given level of growth is the degree to which it corresponds to people's wishes. Despite the fact that most Americans live in metropolitan areas,[1] public opinion surveys indicate a consistent preference for smaller places. A 1970 Gallup Poll, for example, surveyed adult residents of metropolitan centers; according to responses, only 18 percent preferred to live in cities, while 26 percent preferred suburbs, 31 percent preferred small towns, and 24 percent preferred farms (reported in Hoch 1972a:246). Many Americans are thus apparently

not especially happy with their current location—a conclusion supported by an earlier Survey Research Center study
which found that one-quarter of those persons surveyed
would have preferred to live farther away from the center of
the city (Ibid.).[2] These findings were confirmed by a fairly
recent study conducted for the U.S. Commission on Population Growth and the American Future which found the following distribution of preferences among the 1,700 adults
surveyed, relative to actual location:

TABLE 6.1

Attitudes toward City Size

	Where do you live now?	Where would you prefer to live?
Open country	12%	34%
Small town or city	33	30
Medium-sized city or suburb	28	22
Larger city or suburb	27	14
Total	100	100

Source: Finkler, 1972:22

The same study also found that one-quarter of the population in large-sized metropolitan areas think that the city they
live in is too big, while one-half feel that the government
should try to "discourage further growth of large metropolitan
areas" or "try to encourage people and industry to move to
smaller cities and towns" (Ibid.). Similar opinions concerning city size have been found in studies that limited themselves to residents of a single state or even a single metropolitan area (see, for example, Appelbaum, et al. 1976:41–43). A
number of studies also indicate that people's confidence and
satisfaction with local government are higher for smaller governmental units, and that in general people prefer decentral-
ized governmental forms and local autonomy (for a survey
and summary of such studies see Task Force on Local Government Reform 1974:26–28).

NOTES

1. According to the 1970 census, 60.5 percent of the total population lived in Standard Metropolitan Statistical Areas; one-fifth lived in metropolitan areas of a quarter million or more persons (U.S. Dept. of Commerce 1973a.)

2. Nine percent wished they were closer, and 66 percent were happy with their present location.

CHAPTER

7

CONCLUSIONS

This paper has attempted to assess the effects of growth in a comprehensive and standardized fashion, both through comparing the results of previous studies, and undertaking a separate analysis of 115 moderately sized, comparable urban places. In this chapter I shall first summarize the results of these findings, and then offer some general conclusions on the larger body of information reviewed.

SUMMARY OF PRINCIPAL FINDINGS

The most striking finding is that at least for moderately sized places, size and growth effects are minor relative to other influences. In the private sector, larger and faster growing urbanized areas have somewhat higher median family incomes; the fastest growing areas have higher rents and more expensive homes, while the largest areas have slightly higher levels of unemployment. While such effects are persistent, they are considerably attenuated when other influences are

99

taken into account—particularly the age of the central city,
whether or not it is located in the South, and, in the case of
housing costs and unemployment, median family income.
While the combined effects of all influences may account for
as much as four-fifths of the variance in these measures, in no
case does the effect of size and growth—net of other influences—amount to more than 12 percent. With regard to the
measures of crime, a similar pattern emerges; while city size is
positively associated with higher rates of murders-homicides,
robberies-burglaries, and automobile thefts, the association is
substantively weak and is generally reduced by including
other variables. Such variables—particularly the percentage of
blacks and Spanish-American persons in the population, and
the degree to which the city boundaries include the entire
urbanized area—prove to be far more important than size or
growth. Concerning public health, only two of the five indicators (those presumably indexing the degree of social disorganization) prove to have any association with size or
growth at all: the death rate from cirrhosis and the suicide
rate were both found to be higher in the fastest growing
places, once the effects of other variables were taken into
account. Again, however, the relations are substantively
weak, relative to such influences as percent black or Spanish-
American, median age, or region. Finally, looking at the public sector, the results are somewhat ambiguous. The per
capita costs of fire protection are slightly lower in the fastest-
growing places; the costs of police protection are higher; and
payroll costs for personnel common to all cities are somewhat lower in moderately growing places. There are no size
effects per se, once all influences are taken into account.
Growth effects are again minor relative to those of other
variables, which eliminate the differences in fire protection
costs altogether. In the case of the public sector, the principal influence appears to be neither city population nor
growth rate, but the relative size of the surrounding urbanized area population: there is evidence that central-city
taxpayers, to some extent, subsidize suburban commuters
who utilize city services.

The pattern of effects may be summarized as follows:
crime is negatively associated with size; public health is

negatively associated with growth; median income is higher in larger and faster-growing areas, but this is offset by the higher housing costs (and cost of living generally) in such places; and the cost of many city services seems to be lowest in places that are neither losing population nor growing at a rapid rate. But these broad conclusions must be strongly qualified to take into account the reduced magnitude of the associations on which they are based: there are clearly influences stronger than size or growth which affect the quality of life in the cities studied, influences which have been indexed by such variables as racial composition, region, education, and metropolitan "consolidation." Size and growth differentials in the quality of urban life are thus minor, both absolutely and relative to the influence of other factors. These other factors themselves must be regarded as indexes for other social forces of which there is currently an incomplete understanding. The presence of poor blacks and Latinos in central cities, or the exploitation of central-city services by suburban commuters, may be empirically associated with size and growth, and, therefore, help to explain their effects, but a causal relationship between such sets of factors cannot yet be specified.

THE EFFECTS OF SIZE AND GROWTH: SOME GENERAL CONSIDERATIONS

It is clear that speculations about the effects of size and growth of urban areas far exceed the evidence currently available. There is, in general, an absence of theoretical understanding concerning the dynamics of urban growth, and little or no attempt has been made to link what theory there is to empirical research in most studies. Differences which have been observed have to do more with the quality of life than with economic conditions; while air quality, traffic congestion, and crime clearly suffer in larger places relative to smaller ones, few definitive conclusions can be drawn with respect to occupational structure, job availability, or general economic well-being. While the cost of government services, per capita, tends to increase with city size, such differences may in part be due to differences in level and quality of service that are simply not controlled. The higher wage scales available in the largest urban areas indeed provide higher incomes, at least for part of the urban population, but this income advantage is partially offset by higher cost of living, and—perhaps equally important—by the concomitant deterioration in more subjective aspects of the quality of life. Insofar as such deterioration is difficult to quantify in dollar terms, no broad estimate of the net costs or benefits is possible; furthermore, a bias is introduced in favor of that which can be quantified (for example, income differentials), while more "subjective" aspects are accorded secondary treatment (for example, governmental "distance"). Although economists are devoting increased attention to the problem of measuring such "externalities" as pollution and congestion, it is doubtful that these quality-of-life effects are conceptually commensurable with such clearly economic costs and benefits as higher incomes or increased government expenditures.

How does one weigh clean air against the possibility of a higher salary? The excitement of a cosmopolitan atmosphere against hour-long commutes between home and office? The availability of a wide range of specialized service against an increased risk of being mugged or raped? The answer—as Duncan (1951) noted almost 25 years ago—is that it all depends. It depends on whether one is a businessman, looking for a particular range of supporting services; the head of a major corporation, looking for a suitable environment for a suitable environment for a "home office"; a worker, looking for a job and a safe, clean environment in which to raise a family; or a person over 65, looking for a place in which to retire. The economists argue that individuals and firms take all possible factors into account when determining their locational "preferences"; larger places thus offer "compensatory payments" in the form of higher incomes, to offset unfavorable quality-of-life differences. Such reasoning, of course, leads to the conclusion that the existing special allocation of people is somehow optimal, and urges great caution against "well-meaning but misguided" attempts at regulating growth by local governments.

For policy makers concerned with growth management, the studies reviewed—as well as the present study—must be taken as primarily descriptive: while they tell us little concerning the process of growth itself, they do afford an enumeration of some correlates of city size that obtain at the time of the study. It is possibly useful to know such empirical regularities as the fact that larger cities spend more per capita on public services, quality differentials notwithstanding; that commuters spend considerably more time in transit in large metropolitan areas than in medium-sized cities; or that the largest cities may tend to be more economically diversified than smaller ones. But such information bears several important qualifications. First, it must be recognized that knowledge of such regularities tells us nothing about their source or probable future state; in the absence of a theoretical understanding about the dynamics of urban growth in a given network of cities, we can only speculate about future relationships between city size and other variables of interest. Second, it must be noted that whatever the degree of regularity observed, it is the absence of strong regularities that characterizes cities along most dimensions studied: There are numerous exceptions to any observed relationship between city size and any postulated correlate of size. This is particularly important for the policy maker to consider; it indicates that there is no such thing as an "optimal city size" for all cities and all persons. This is not just because the notion of optimum involves value considerations, as Duncan (1951: 772) correctly observed; it is also because each city faces its own unique set of conditions, even if the values to be optimized can be agreed upon. For example, while governmental costs generally increase more rapidly than population as a city grows, for a city that has already invested in substantial expansion of its capital infrastructure, some growth may actually reduce per capita expenditures by spreading high fixed costs over larger numbers of persons. In other words, descriptive studies can serve to alert us to regularities that customarily obtain among large numbers of cities; the stronger the regularity, the higher the probability of its incidence in any particular city. But the planner seeking to understand the consequences of growth in his or her city will ultimately have to undertake a concrete analysis of that city.

Finally, it should be firmly remembered that even the strongest of observed relationships are neither natural nor inevitable. If, for example, city size and crime rates are associated today, that association is produced by the actions of persons who together build a society that permits widespread unemployment, inferior opportunities, and hence high crime rates to concentrate among minority groups in large metropolitan areas. Similarly, a society commited to automobiles as the principal mode of transport, and which is unwilling to force automobile manufacturers to internalize the costs of pollution control, guarantees that large cities will have congested streets and dirty air. But these relationships represent decisions—decisions by governmental officials to tolerate certain levels of unemployment or underemployment as "acceptable," decisions by highway planners and politicians to continue to subsidize the private car through highway trust funds, decisions by automobile manufacturers to place profits over health and safety in importance. Should other decisions be made, the observed relationships will change. It is possible to have densely populated cities with virtually no crime and pollution (and few cars), if that is what is desired. Such a result can be achieved, but only insofar as the economic and political conditions that give rise to the current relationships among these variables are intelligently altered. And such alteration, in turn, presupposes an adequate conceptual understanding of the underlying processes that shape our urban areas.

8

AFTERWORD: SOME THEORETICAL SPECULATIONS
ON THE DYNAMICS OF URBAN GROWTH

In the introductory chapter I noted that the present research strategy was dictated by the exigencies of policy
formation, and, as a consequence, lacked an explicit theoretical framework. It was therefore limited to describing the correlates and consequences of urban growth as if population
size and increase were themselves explanatory or causal
variables. In this final chapter I shall attempt to get behind
such demographic variables, elaborating a theoretical orienta-
tion which will account for various aspects of urban life in
terms of an underlying dynamic, of which population size
and increase are partial indicators. The argument to be made,
in general terms, is this: neither size nor growth is an independent cause of changes in indicators of the public or private economy, of health, or of crime. Rather, size and growth
are themselves consequences of other processes that shape
our cities—processes which, in fact, account for observed
changes in the social and economic indicators. In some instances size and growth may be regarded as intervening variables in the dynamic, in that concentrations of population in

an urban area play a key role; in other instances they are merely a gloss for processes which operate irrespective of urban concentrations.

In elaborating this argument, I shall be drawing upon a framework which is itself only partially elaborated: It does not yet constitute a theory, having been advanced in different forms by divergent writers who only loosely may be said to share a common sociological paradigm. It therefore suffers the flaws of eclecticism; nonetheless, I believe it affords promise in enabling us to understand the dynamics and consequences of U.S. urban concentration. The writers whose influences are most clearly felt in what follows include Harvey (1973, 1974, 1975), Mollenkopf (1977), Molotch (1976), Lamarche (1976), and particularly Lojkine (1976) and Castells (1976, 1977); a useful collection of essays which develop the framework is found in Pickvance (1976). I shall develop the argument through a series of stages: first, I shall describe the setting within which urban growth occurs; next, the fundamental dynamic; third, the historical dynamic; and finally, current consequences for urban life.

THE FRAMEWORK OF URBAN GROWTH

Urban growth in the United States reflects the requirements of capitalist economic growth; it constitutes the principal spatial manifestation of such growth. U.S. capitalism in the mid-twentieth century has the following general features which will prove relevant in the ensuing discussion: (1) production for private profit; (2) private ownership of capital; and (3) limited extension of state activities into the private sector, particularly at the local level. Each of these features bears brief elaboration.

Production for Profit

Profitability criteria govern the vast majority of decisions made by productive enterprises. Goods are not produced to satisfy requirements of consumers per se (although such requirements are always presupposed in production); rather, they are produced so as to maximize the firm's profits. Firms are thus confronted with a set of requirements which must be satisfied if profits are to be sustained; these entail marketing considerations on the one hand and production costs on the other. Productive firms are under continued pressure to adopt strategies which guarantee their products will be purchased (involving communications and transportation technology) and which cut costs (particularly the costs of labor). We shall see, momentarily, that such strategies entail the spatial concentration of people and infrastructure, that is, the urban form.

Private Ownership

Since capital in the United States is privately owned, the owners of capital must make decisions in the face of competition and, hence, uncertain market considerations—although empirically these may be partially mitigated by strong tendencies toward centralization and concentration of ownership. To the extent that individual capital must make investment decisions in the face of competition and uncertainty, the shape of overall capitalist development will be unplanned. This anarchic quality of market-generated growth is seen, in spatial form, in the mosaic of land-use patterns that comprise the urban area. Of particular interest in the ensuing argument is the effect on urbanization of several principal forms of capital, whose interests will often diverge. The competition among different forms of capital will provide a key to understanding the configurations of urban space.

Limited Direct State Intervention

In the United States, and particularly at the local level, there is relatively little direct intervention by government in the processes of production. With few exceptions the state does not enter directly in the production of housing or urban infrastructure; rather, its historic role has been to help main-

tain a favorable climate for capital accumulation. This has
been achieved largely through various activities relating to
the financing of private investment—the setting of interest
rates or regulation of the banking industry. The state is also
called upon to respond to conditions that threaten capital
accumulation; the various public programs of the past decade
may be seen as the response of the state to the urban unrest
of the period. In general, there has been no tradition of enforced urban planning in the United States, and few mechanisms by which such planning might be implemented at
the local level exist.

THE UNDERLYING DYNAMICS
OF URBAN GROWTH

Urban growth thus occurs within a framework of
capitalist accumulation, involving production for profit,
private ownership, and a restricted state role. Capital accumulation requires sustained profits; this, in turn, requires that
the mass of goods produced realize their value as articles of
consumption. In order to maximize profits and, hence,
further accumulation, capital must simultaneously strive to
minimize production costs while maximizing commodity
consumption. It is this double imperative that links capital
accumulation with urbanization.

Urbanization entails spatial concentration: concentration of people, resources, and infrastructure. The benefits of
such concentration for capitalist production were readily
apparent a century ago: the concentration of workers and
machinery in a single workhouse contributed significantly to
productive efficiency, as did the concentration of a general
work force in a single urban labor market. The initial economies of such concentration had to do with lowering the costs
of production: both labor and capital could be more ef-
ficiently exploited to the extent that their scale was increased.
Additionally, however, another economy resulted from spatial
concentration—that of enhanced communication: insofar as
capitalist production requires coordination among separate
agencies, such coordination is facilitated by their concentra-

tion in space. But production is not the only concern in capital accumulation. Commodities, once produced, must find their way to consumers. This entails storage, transport, merchandising, and retailing operations. It is useful to distinguish two broad functions that must be satisfied: in the process of capital accumulation: production and circulation, the latter including both the circulation of money (finance) and commodities (commerce). The efficiency of circulation, as well as production, was enhanced through spatial concentration of these functions, and the urban form under capitalist production initially reflected circulation efficiencies.

Following the depression of the 1930s, cities came to acquire yet another function of increasing importance to capital accumulation—the stimulation of consumption in the face of chronic tendencies toward lagging demand. Harvey (1975:139) notes that "the American city is now designed to stimulate consumption. The emphasis on sprawl, individualized modes of consumption, owner-occupancy, and the like, is to be interpreted as one of several responses to the underconsumption problems of the 1930s. . . . " He thus sees cities as increasingly serving as "consumption artifacts" rather than "workshops" (Ibid.). It is useful in this regard to distinguish two forms of consumption promoted by the urban form—individual and collective consumption. While the former is commonly associated with the highly privatized, commodity-oriented lifestyle of the U.S. population, it is the latter that has assumed increasing significance in recent years. Lojkine (1976:121) defines "collective means of consumption" as "the totality of material supports of the activities devoted to the extended reproduction of material labor power, which is not to be confused with simple physiological reproduction or with the consumption-destruction by an individual of a material object." This last phrase refers to the collective character of such consumption: both the needs and the manner of consumption are inherently social. "Concretely," Lojkine notes, "this refers today to the totality of medical, sports, educational, cultural, and public transport facilities"; elsewhere, he includes some forms of housing as an instance.

The costs of collective consumption are largely borne by the state, which is seen as the principal provider of such facilities. While these facilities are essential to the reproduction of the customary lifestyle of the work force, they constitute legitimate expectations concerning an adequate "quality of life," and they also tend to be unprofitable; hence, they are socialized. While capital is thus able to slough off the cost of providing such facilities (which would otherwise constitute a deduction from profits), such costs return indirectly in the form of taxes and inflation. Whether such indirect costs are deducted from profits, thereby impeding accumulation, will depend on the ability of capital to pass them forward in the form of higher commodity prices to consumers. Collective consumption, like individual consumption, is both source and consequences of urbanization, due to efficiencies of concentration.

Urban spatial concentration is thus a necessary consequence of capitalist economic accumulation, entailing the production and sales of commodities, the circulation of capital, and the reproduction of the lifestyle of the work force. This does not explain, however, why urban areas take on particular forms—why they follow certain growth trajectories, or are plagued by certain environmental, social, economic, and political problems. To understand these latter processes it is necessary to first identify the principal parties to the production and reproduction processes, identifying the separate interests of each. Then we will be in a position to examine recent urbanization in the United States. It is useful to group the agents of urban growth into three broad categories: capital, the work force, and the state. Each of these will be briefly considered in turn.

Capital

Capital can be divided into several principal fractions, whose often conflicting interests in large part determine the dynamic of urban growth. Industrial capital, directly engaged in commodity production, seeks to minimize production costs while maximizing market demand for its products.

It thus has an interest in locating where the factors of production are cheapest (principally land and labor), which has meant a movement in recent years away from the central city (where such economies were realized previously) to suburban or peripheral locations. Urban growth may exact excessive costs from industrial capital—both in the form of rising production costs, if growth entails an increase in the price of land or in workers' living costs (resulting in upward pressures on wages) and in the form of "inconvenience costs" such as traffic congestion, pollution, crime, and so forth. Such "inconvenience costs" may assume a direct monetary form, when public intervention is necessary to deal with their sources; rising taxes then subtract from profitability. On the other hand, the maintenance and enhancement of aggregate demand encourages continued spatial concentration of markets, as do economies in the circulation of commodities once produced. Hence, industrial capital is likely to favor continuing growth and concentration in general, although its position on local growth will depend on the particular economies and diseconomies that will result.

Commercial capital realizes its profits through the distribution of goods already produced. Retail and wholesale activities, advertising, marketing, and the transportation of goods all fall under this heading; their costs generally constitute a deduction from the profits of industrial capital—a cost of production—and industrial capital is therefore interested in any economies of location which minimize such costs. It is clear that commercial capital benefits in this regard from population concentration and the augmented markets (and distribution economies) that result. On the other hand, all commercial capital does not benefit equally from growth. Extremely small retail outlets—"mom and pop stores"—service a highly localized market area (for example, a neighborhood), and thus benefit little from overall urban growth; they do, however, directly experience the "inconvenience costs" as well as higher taxes which may result. On the other hand, large-scale merchandising enterprises—chain stores, department stores, and so forth—usually serve extensive market areas and benefit considerably from urban concentration. This group includes the largest locally based com-

mercial concerns, as well as extra-local ones. It constitutes
one of the principal mainstays of what Molotch (1976) terms
the "local growth machine" and may be identified with the
"downtown business interests," although the largest extra-
local concerns—which serve regional markets—may encourage
peripheral development in direct competition with the downtown business district.

Landed capital is another mainstay of the local growth
machine; it includes all those who own real estate for profit-
making purposes. Landed capital can range in size from small
holders who maintain a few rental units for retirement income, to extremely large developers who are among the most
visible proponents of growth, and who benefit most directly.
Because land constitutes a resource central to all forms of
capital as well as to the consumption of the work force,
landed capital occupies a key position in the dynamics of the
urban spatial form. The price of urban land constitutes a deduction from the profits of the other forms of capital that
must rent land, and, hence, figures as a direct cost of production; it also constitutes a major component of the cost of
living, and, hence, figures into the price of labor. Furthermore, unlike other investments, land is spatially "fixed":
location is an attribute of land, and thus enters into its price.

Rent thus reflects locational considerations, of which
three are most important: (a) the advantages of a piece of
property which depend exclusively upon its site in relation to
neighboring private or public land uses; (b) the advantages of
a piece of property which depend upon its internal organization and the benefits of coordination or communication this
confers upon its occupants (as with a shopping plaza or redevelopment project); and (c) the advantages of a piece of
property which reflect its anticipated future use relative to
likely urbanization trends on neighboring property. The three
different types of rent associated with these three advantages
are termed differential rent I, differential rent II, and absolute
rent, respectively (see Lamarche 1976:100–109 for further
elaboration). The effect of landownership on urban development differs according to the type of rent received, since the
three different types of rent entail different interests. Inasmuch as the two forms of differential rent are maximized

through the greatest development of property relative to its locational attributes, landowners seeking this type of rent will seek to develop their property to its "highest and best use." In particular, since differential rent II is maximized through land assembly and the reorganization of spatial form within a single piece of property, it depends only partly on the accidents of locational advantage: large-scale land development thus constitutes a major avenue available to landed capital by which returns can be maximized, and such capital then has a significant interest in acquiring land and developing it fully and rationally. This is one of the principal forms through which the urban planning function is able to occur in the United States.

On the other hand, where once profitable property has lost part of its locational advantage in terms of its current use due to changing urban form—as is typically the case with old housing near the urban center—profitability takes the form of absolute rent; in this case the land itself contains the value, and its existing development is of reduced or even negligible importance. Landowners of such property are, therefore, under economic constraints to withhold development until anticipated changes in surrounding land use maximize returns; property is thus allowed to deteriorate, contributing to the social problems which attend such "urban blight." Just as the possibility of realizing differential rent II constitutes a major impetus to private attempts to rationally plan the urban form, so does the promise of absolute rent inhibit such efforts: land is speculatively withheld from the market, creating scarcity, driving up prices on remaining property, and contributing to urban decay.

Since smaller landowners are less likely to be able to amass the capital necessary for large-scale development, they are more likely to strive for the purely locational advantages associated with differential rent I and absolute rent; this may constitute a real impediment to local efforts by developers at private planning and thereby contribute to the patchwork irrationality of the city. On the other hand, since planned large-scale development is able to realize a high level of rent (differential rent II), it does not benefit everybody equally. In particular, the high rents will be afforded by those who

directly benefit from the locational and organizational advantages conferred by the development; these include major
commercial and financial interests, for whom externalities
constitute a significant economic advantage and wealthy
residents willing to pay a premium for convenience and status.
Small retail establishments and persons of modest or low income receive few such advantages, and, hence, cannot afford
the high rents. Their interests are most antagonistic to landed
capital, since they are most at its mercy; as landed capital
becomes increasingly concentrated in the hands of major
developers—through market forces or public redevelopment
programs—small businesses and marginal workers are the first
casualties.

In general, to the extent that the ownership of land is
widely scattered, the interests of landed capital as a whole
will interfere with those of the other fractions of capital.
Private land ownership cross-cuts the need of capital to flow
freely to the most advantageous locations or to reduce the
costs of labor through reducing the cost of its reproduction.
On the other hand, the increasing concentration of landed
capital permits more rational land use from the point of view
of the other capital fractions, although at the expense of
smaller capital and the work force.

Financial capital constitutes the fourth and final form
of capital, and the most significant in understanding postwar
urbanization. This form—which includes, broadly, commercial
banks, savings and loan institutions, and life insurance and
pension funds—bankrolls urban growth; it thus serves the
function of mediation between the various uses of land. Harvey (1975:141; see also 1974), for example, argues that "the
financial superstructure serves to coordinate the urbanization
process in a particular locale with the overall aggregative push
towards stimulating effective demand and facilitating capital
accumulation": finance capital thus has a highly generalized
interest in growth. Since all the other fractions of capital are
to a degree dependent on finance capital for sources of funds,
it has a stake in their overall health. Finance capital also has
particular interests, represented in its portfolio of investments. Thus, in addition to promoting growth in general,
finance capital must take care to secure investments already

taken. For example, Harvey (1975:157–58) cites evidence to show that perhaps one-quarter of all mortgage debt is held against inner-city properties—a figure which is increased substantially if other forms of debt are also considered (that is, debt secured against property taxes and debts assumed by public and private utilities). The deterioration of the inner cities thus has severe implications for the financial structure and—because of the centrality of finance capital—for the economy as a whole. This is why the maintenance of the central cities is of such major public as well as private concern.

The interests of finance capital are long-term. Mortgages are typically written for 30 or 40 years, and often on the assumption of continuing urban growth (Harvey 1975:137). Thus, finance capital, more than any other form, often assumes the "planning function" within the market economy. However, since finance capital itself is highly uncoordinated, consisting of numerous private institutions (many of which are small and locally based) as well as the public agencies which mediate capital flows, coordination is minimal, and the adverse consequences often striking. Suburbanization, for example, represented an extremely important outlet for capital following World War II but its consequences now threaten older capital investment in the central cities. The interests of finance capital may also run counter to those of the other capital fractions. Debt service constitutes a major component of the cost of land and other forms of property, costs which are passed along in the form of higher rent and prices; from the perspective of industrial capital, such costs constitute a deduction from profits, and may impede accumulation. Increasingly, however, the interests of finance capital and those of the largest industrial, commercial, and landed capital are becoming harmonized, as there is evidence that the latter are being absorbed by the former (Lojkine 1976: 138). To the extent that this is the case in any particular locality, local growth may be expected to assume a more planned character intended to maximize externalitites and reduce costs for capitalists as a whole; smaller capitals, however, will not necessarily share in such benefits.

The Work Force

While stable workers may benefit to a degree from the economics of spatial concentration, they also clearly bear the burden of whatever diseconomies also follow. Such diseconomies may be felt as "inconvenience costs," direct costs in the form of higher prices for housing and other components of the cost of living or taxes to pay for increased state intervention necessitated by growth. Insofar as is possible, capital will seek to sustain profits by passing costs along to consumers; it is thus at this level where the squeeze is most acutely felt. On the other hand, insofar as the work force expects a certain standard of consumption to be maintained, the rising cost of living will give rise to pressures for higher wages—which threaten profitability.

In addition to the stable work force, urban areas are the principal repositories for marginally employed, underemployed, or unemployed persons whose maintenance costs have increasingly fallen on the state. This surplus working population constitutes a reservoir from which low-paying, low-status positions can be recruited; it serves also to keep wages depressed in non-unionized sectors of the local economy. On the other hand, this population is the most politically volatile part of the work force. Maintaining the peace among the surplus population is therefore a principal cost of urban concentration—whether it takes the form of police protection against the higher crime rates that prevail in this group, government transfers and programs aimed at placating the poorest, or the costs of containing open riots and rebellions. These costs are to an extent socialized in the form of higher taxes, which are felt by business as a deduction from profits and by the stable work force as a deduction from income. The costs of "urban blight" are directly experienced as location diseconomies for businesses situated near concentrations of the urban poor.

The State Sector

Local government serves the function of mediating between the various interests represented by the different fractions of capital, while socializing the costs of collective consumption. It, thus, has the classic role of system maintenance, a role difficult to perform in light of the conflicting interests and unequal powers it confronts. Local government is increasingly called upon to assist in the provision of schools, low-cost housing, recreational facilities, cultural centers, and public transportation. The different fractions of capital have different interests in seeing such costs socialized. Industrial capital, for example, seeks to minimize the costs of reproduction of the work force, inasmuch as such costs are reflected in wage demands; it therefore benefits by having such costs borne by the state. Financial capital and landed capital seek to minimize the risks associated with investment in real estate, and thus have an interest in governmental activities that promote residential stability (for example, zoning) and neighborhood preservation—although this may in particular instances be offset by the possibility of realizing absolute rent through speculative practices. Large-scale commercial capital has an interest in maintaining access to markets, leading to pressures on local government for redevelopment, urban renewal, and highway construction between the periphery and the downtown. Any conflicts of interest between different fractions of capital will be played out in the public arena.

While local government is engaged in system maintenance, it is not thereby an imparital arbiter of interests. In the first place, the work force—and particularly the surplus working population—is likely to have very little influence in local government; its influence is brought to bear in the form of direct political actions (for example, rent strikes and riots) which force the local government to respond with ameliorative programs. The costs of system management are increasingly high and tend to devolve disproportionately on the stable working population—either in the form of direct taxation (property taxes) or indirect levies (business taxes, which are passed on to consumers). The "middle class" is thus caught in the squeeze, a situation which has gone far to undermine the credibility and hence legitimacy of local government in recent years.

In the second place, public employees in areas such as police and fire protection, education, and social services have in some cases been able to maintain job security or desired wage levels through militant action. As governmental workers themselves acquire a voice in setting governmental policies—even if that voice is restricted to work-related demands—they can be seen as exerting an independent force. One immediate consequence has been a downward inflexibility of the size and cost of growing public bureaucracies—a cost passed on in the form of higher taxes on businesses and the middle classes, and one which has contributed to the fiscal insolvency of some cities.

THE HISTORICAL RESOLUTION

Thus far I have considered the dynamics underlying growth—and the principal parties involved—in abstraction; the particular configuration of forces will reflect empirical conditions. It is difficult to generalize across communities, although some broad developments over recent years seem common to many. Let me briefly summarize one set of those developments which seem to me to be of particular importance for understanding the growth of certain key urban areas.

In the period following World War II, partly in response to sluggish economic recovery, the federal government promoted the surburbanization of the urban population. This was achieved by a number of indirect mechanisms, chief of which were a system of mortgage guarantees—which stabilized private investment in the housing industry and thereby promoted home ownership—and the highway trust fund, which subsidized an unending spiral of freeway construction. These policies were particularly beneficial to landed and financial capital, but all of capital benefited to an extent from the fomenting of a middle-class lifestyle based on extended, privatized consumption. The shape of many urban areas, however, has come to reflect the short-sightedness of such policies. On the one hand the costs of urban sprawl (traffic congestion, air pollution, extended home-to-work travel time) were experienced by all persons throughout these urban areas, on the other, their central business district experienced a loss of industry, jobs, and stable work force to the periphery.

This flight of persons and industries in these places was particularly damaging to financial capital, landed capital, some commercial capital, and, to a lesser extent, to industrial capital. To the extent that directive functions required concentration and communication, home offices, banks, and subsidiary functions such as marketing remained "trapped" in deteriorating urban cores, surrounded by an increasingly restive surplus population. Declining land values adversely affected both landowners and the financial institutions who held the mortgages, leading one congressional committee to conclude that "continued central-city deterioration would lead to the devaluation of these assets with serious repercussions within the national financial structure" (cited in Harvey 1975:158). The push for redevelopment of the downtown areas, which began in earnest with the rise of the "pro-growth coalitions" in many cities in the sixties (Mollenkopf, 1977), was the principal response on the part of the downtown business interests in many major cities. Redevelopment sought to displace marginal businesses, deteriorated housing, and the urban surplus working population with a planned central business district. Scattered, privately owned parcels of land were assembled by local governmental agencies with the help of federal funding; the lands thus assembled were made available to large-scale developers at a substantial write-down in price. Developers were then able to plan for a mixture of projects which would maximize the externalities associated with the redevelopment area, making it extremely attractive to prospective tenants and resulting in high rents (differential rent II) which effectively priced most small businesses out of the area and its environs. Such redevelopment areas constituted a form of urban planning on the part of major financial, commercial, and landed capital. The patchwork of small businesses, low-income housing, and widely scattered landholdings that previously had characterized the downtown core of cities whose redevelopment was successfully implemented was replaced by a carefully arranged mosaic of luxury housing, expensive retail outlets, cultural facilities, sports arenas, trade centers, and corporate headquarters. The costs of redevelopment were socialized; federal grants, local tax revenues, and locally provided infrastructure helped reduce initial costs to the developers in the expectation of substantial future returns. Such costs were to be compensated, in theory, through the expected enlarged tax base which would eventually result. In some places, where access to the downtown was felt to be a problem, freeways or public transportation systems were also built to link the redeveloped area with the affluent suburbs; this entailed additional land acquisition and subsidized expenditures.

It is difficult to assess the overall success of the redevelopment strategy. Its failure in many cities was due to a mixture of factors not yet clearly understood, although two stand out as of special significance. First, the urban surplus working population—principally black and Latino—became increasingly volatile during the sixties. Their numbers swollen by postwar migrations from the rural South, highly segregated urban racial minorities found neither jobs nor a better life in the cities. These groups also suffered diredly at the hands of the redevelopers, who reduced available housing stock, displaced small businesses, and destroyed neighborhood. The response— the urban unrest of the sixties—led to the discovery of the "urban problem" and the attempts on the part of the federal government at its resolution. While the poverty programs succeeded in establishing local bureaucracies and in some cases training indigenous leaders, they failed to eliminate urban poverty; they did, however, leave a legacy of governmental intervention which was to prove exceedingly costly to local governments in the seventies. The mobilization of segments of the urban population in the sixties constituted a significant barrier to continued redevelopment in many places; by the seventies these had coalesced into urban social movements in some cities, which were able to effectively challenge the political power of the growth coalitions (see Castells 1976:21–26; 1977). A second reason for the failure of redevelopment lies in the economic stagnation of the past decade. Redevelopment was based on the assumption of continued economic growth, with steadily rising purchasing power and, hence, expanded markets for downtown business; the erosion of purchasing power, therefore, undermined the viability of many projects. Additionally, the costs of the poverty programs of the sixties increasingly devolved on localities under the economic policies of the Nixon and Ford administrations. Cities were caught in a tightening vise, confronted simultaneously by a declining tax base and rising costs of urban services. One response to this pinch—increasing local taxes—contributed to the flight of businesses and property owners, further diminishing the tax base. Another response—paying for programs through short-term indebtedness—mortgaged some cities to large financial institutions, with the consequences seen dramatically in New York City. At the present, many cities appear to be caught in a trap of ongoing concentrated poverty, populations increasingly hostile to the redevelopment strategy, financial insolvency, and downtown business and financial interests who continue to have a major stake in reestablishing the viability of the urban area.

THE EFFECTS OF "URBAN GROWTH"

By now it should be evident that "growth effects" are considerably more complex than their reduction to demographic causes would suggest. In this concluding section I will attempt to suggest an approach to studying the effects of "urban growth," in light of the analytical distinctions and historical developments elucidated in this chapter.

The Postwar Development of U.S. Cities

We have seen how continued urban growth is a consequence of the drive for profit maximization in a market economy. Growth—which entails the concentration of population and economic activities in urban space—is necessitated because of the economies it brings; externalities, enhanced rents, circulation efficiencies, the stimulation of consumption, and efficiencies in collective consumption all benefit different fractions of capital. Because of communication efficiencies and economies of scale which follow from concentration, urbanized areas have been the principal historical vehicle by which such economies could be obtained.

But given the unplanned character of U.S. capitalism, urban development has been uneven. In many cases, central cities have been filled with working people searching for jobs, many of whom are unskilled immigrants from the rural South, and a substantial proportion of whom are from racial minorities. At the same time, governmental policy—aimed at stimulating consumption—has promoted the development of the periphery, and urban industry has increasingly fled the core, attracted by the prospects of a more stable work force, lower rents, and reduced taxes. Industrial and financial capital have in the short run benefited from the suburbanization of the stable working population, but at the long-run cost of abandoning the central cities to a volatile stratum of the population. And, insofar as the economic interests of capital remain tied to the central cities, this uneven development is adversely felt by capital as well as by the urban poor.

This process of uneven development can be loosely seen as one key developmental type characterizing the postwar urbanization experience of many American cities. This type entails the sequence of events previously described: immigration, suburbanization, redevelopment, the rise of urban protest movements, and so forth. The underlying dynamics reflect the struggle for profits on the part of the different fractions of capital, the nature of state intervention in the interests of guaranteeing sustained capital accumulation, and the response of the urban population to the conditions they face. It is important to note that what is being offered here is not a model encompassing all urban development, but rather an approach to developing such a model. I have chosen to focus on a particular developmental type because of its significance for a number of major American cities; there are, however, other patterns which could be similarly typified. The type present is of special importance, however, because it expresses the most important and general postwar patterns of private investment in urban areas, of urban public policy, and of popular response. Those urban areas whose development can be appropriately characterized according to this type will, of course, deviate from the type in significant ways as a consequence of their particular characteristics. They will share some of those characteristics with other areas that are similarly situated either geographically or historically. For example, the physical structure of the older Northeastern cities reflects their common experience with industrialization at the turn of the century, during a period when agglomeration economics were of central importance; the physical structure of the Sunbelt cities, on the other hand, is the result of much more recent industrialization, during a period when spatial decentralization was both technologically feasible and economically desirable. Such baseline historical influences must themselves be overlaid on the unique biographical characteristics of each city: for example, the degree of cohesion or "far-sightedness" on the part of its business community, and the influence of that community with major corporate investors and federal policy makers; or, the degree of organization and militancy of its working population. Thus, the actual history of any urban area can be understood as the intersection of three factors: a developmental one, entailing very broad public and private strategies to secure an adequate level of capital accumulation, and popular responses to the costs of those strategies; a baseline historical one, reflecting the period in which the locality developed the major features of its industrial base and physical structure; and a biographical one, containing the many "accidental" characteristics peculiar to the locality.

If this line of reasoning is correct, then size and growth effects can be respecified in terms of the dynamic resulting from the intersection of these three factors. While there is possibly a loose correlation between the demographic variables and the more fundamental ones,[1] the influence of size and growth *per se* should disappear once the underlying dynamic is taken into account. By way of illustration, I shall reconsider some of the principal size and growth effects previously analyzed, in light of the ideal developmental type that has been presented.

The Private Sector

While in theory unemployment rates should be equalized among urban areas over time as a result of labor mobility, there may, in fact, be some structural impediments to such equalization. A uniformly high national unemployment rate may discourage relocation, given the low probability of an unemployed person's finding a job elsewhere; furthermore, the increased availability of government transfers may cushion the impact of unemployment and, hence, further diminish the likelihood of continued migration. To the extent that labor is immobile, the local unemployment rate will reflect the degree to which the urban area has served as a magnet for postwar migration streams of marginally employable persons. Such streams will partially have been in response to local patterns of economic growth, with the most rapidly growing areas proving the most attractive to migrants; shifts in regional spending patterns by the federal government (as with defense-related industries) has been one important determinant of such growth patterns. Public and private investment together determine economic growth in a locality; the extent of such growth in turn determines the attractiveness of a locality to potential immigrants. It is possible that urban areas with sizeable, diversified, or rapidly growing economies appear most promising to immigrants as the prospects of finding employment may seem most hopeful in such places. If this is true, then we may expect such places to serve as stronger magnets than others, drawing migrants in numbers disproportionate to the actually available employment opportunities. If, indeed, labor is imperfectly mobile, then unemployment rates in such places may remain somewhat higher; the same should be true of concentration of poverty.

Within urban areas, the distribution between center and peripheral unemployment should be particularly revealing of the areas' developmental stage. More developed areas should have experienced a shift in stable employment to the suburbs, leaving concentrations of unemployed persons in the city core. This should be reflected in higher unemployment rates in the central city than in the urban areas as a whole, as well as higher proportions of the population living in poverty. The same should be true of income, with higher average income levels in the suburban areas of more developed places where the stable work force is increasingly concentrated. The higher overall average income figures observed for larger, more rapidly growing urban areas may reflect the higher average income levels in the suburbs of such relatively "mature" places: it may also reflect a greater concentration of commercial, industrial, or financial wealth. On the other hand, it is also likely that the higher cost of living in larger places must be partially compensated by higher incomes to make such places attractive. One major cause of the higher living cost in larger, faster-growing urban areas is found to be higher property values, reflected in both housing prices and rents. One of the principal functions of concentration is to enhance the economic value of space; this is reflected in differential rent gradients which become steeper as urban areas become larger and more concentrated. In addition, land scarcity is proportional to degree of urbanization, contributing to high land prices in the most urbanized areas, and absolute rents may also be realized in those areas likely to undergo future urbanization. Here again it is important to bear in mind that while property value, size and growth may go hand-in-hand, the underlying cause of the relationship has to do with the realization of rent in a speculative market: profit maximization by landed capital is achieved by taking fullest advantage of concentration economies associated with size and growth under market conditions.

Social and Physical Environment

More developed urban areas have undergone considerable social disorganization as a result of capital flows in search of profits. Such places have experienced an influx of migrants and their subsequent segregation on the basis of skills and racial characteristics; the uprooting of people and the destruction of neighborhoods by highways and redevelopment projects; various forms of urban strife; concentrated poverty and unemployment; physical squalor, partly as a consequence of disincentives to property investment (occa-

sionally the result of the unprofitability of inner-city housing, but also the result of speculation and absolute rent);
and—in general—haphazard patterns of urbanization in which
the urban poor are the real victims. It is not surprising that
more urbanization places have higher levels of crime or
higher indexes of illness, as is found to be the case with
fastest-growing places where these processes are the most
focused. The deterioration of the physical environment can
be similarly explained in terms of capital flows; suburban
sprawl, automobile congestion, pollution, and delapidated
housing are all the consequences of private decisions and public policies aimed at stimulating consumption, reducing production and circulation costs, and, hence, maximizing profits.
While size and growth are associated with these problems,
they do not cause them. Rather, size, growth, and the asso-
ciate problems are best understood as the consequence of the
underlying developmental dynamic.

The Public Sector

The U-shaped curve for the cost of governmental services suggests that economies of scale in service delivery may
be optimized for moderately sized cities. Nonetheless, it is
likely that here, also, developmental patterns are highly important. The most developed cities have experienced the
effects of uneven urbanization, the costs for which have increasingly fallen on local government. Such an interpretation
is consistent with the finding that service costs are higher in
the fastest-growing places; it is in such places where the
effects of uneven growth are most acutely felt.

CONCLUSION

The relationship between size, growth, and urban development is not yet understood; the reflections in this
chapter are merely meant to be suggestive. It is clear, however, that our understanding of urban problems will not be

advanced by continued focus on purely demographic characteristics as the key explanatory variables. Urban processes
occur within a larger framework of capital accumulation—of
the production of wealth and the reproduction of the factors
of production; they are distinguished from this larger framework by virtue of their localization in space. The complex
relationship between the components of capital accumulation
and the economics of spatial concentration provides the key
for understanding the nature and consequences of urban
development. A fuller understanding, however, will have to
await further research based explicitly on theoretical models
which specify with some precision the nature of these relationships.

NOTE

1. For example, controlling on baseline historical influences
(region and period of initial industrialization might be crude indices)
and ignoring unique biographical characteristics, size might be found
to loosely correlate with stage of development, while rate of growth
might show an inverse correlation.

BIBLIOGRAPHY

Advisory Commission on Intergovernmental Relations (ACIR)
  1968   *Urban and Rural America: Policies for Future Growth.*
          Washington, D.C.: U.S. Government Printing Office.

Alonso, William
  1973   "Urban Zero Population Growth." *Daedelus* 102:4
          (Fall):191-206.

Andrews, F. M., J. N. Morgan, and J. A. Sondquist
  1973   *Multiple Classification Analysis.* Ann Arbor: University
          of Michigan.

Appelbaum, Richard
  1976   "City Size and Urban Life: A Preliminary Inquiry Into
          Some Consequences of Growth in American Cities."
          Urban Affairs Quarterly (December).

Appelbaum, Richard, Jennifer Bigelow, Henry Kramer, Harvey Molotch,
and Paul Relis
  1974   *Santa Barbara: The Impacts of Growth.* 3 vols. Santa
          Barbara, California: City of Santa Barbara.
  1976   *The Effects of Urban Growth: A Population Impact
          Analysis.* New York: Praeger.

Bachman, J.
  1970   "The Impact of Family Background and Intelligence
          on Tenth Grade Boys." Ann Arbor: University of
          Michigan Institute for Survey Research.

Baker, C. Ashmore
  1910   "Population and Cost in Relation to City Manage-
          ment." *The Journal of the Royal Statistical Society*
          (December):139-48.

Baum, Paul
    1971   *Issues in Optimal City Size.* U.C.L.A.: Graduate
                School of Management.

Beckham, Barry
    1973   "Some Temporal and Spatial Aspects of Interurban
                Industrial Differentiation." *Social Forces* 51:4 (June):
                462-70.

Berry, Brian J. L. et al.
    1974   "Land Use Forms and the Environment." Paper No.
                155. In *Land Use, Urban Form, and Environmental
                Quality, Final Report.* Chicago: Department of
                Geography Research.

Betz, D. Michael
    1972   "The City as a System Generating Income Equality."
                Social Forces 51:2 (December):192-98.

Blau, Peter, and Otis D. Duncan
    1973   *The American Occupational Structure.* New York:
                Wiley.

Bollens, John C., and Henry J. Schmandt
    1965   *The Metropolis: Its People, Politics, and Economic
                Life.* New York: Harper & Row.

Bolt, Beranek and Newman, Inc.
    1970   *Chicago Urban Noise Study.* Report No. 1411-13.
                Downers Grove, Illinois.

Boulder Area Growth Study Commission
    1973   *Exploring Options for the Future: A Study of
                Growth in Boulder County.* Boulder, Colorado.

Bradley, Richard C.
    1973   *The Costs of Urban Growth: Observations and Judg-
                ments.* Pikes Peak, Colo.: Pikes Peak Area Council
                of Governments.

Braverman, Harry
    1974   *Labor and Monopoly Capital: The Degradation of
                Work in the Twentieth Century.* New York: Monthly
                Review Press.

Brazer, Harvey E.
      1959   "City Expenditures in the United States." Occasional
                   paper 66. New York: National Bureau of Economic
                   Research.

Calhoun, J. B.
      1962   "Population Density and Social Pathology. *Scientific
                   American* 206:2 (February):139-48.

Castells, Manuel
      1976   "The Wild City." *Kapitalistate* 4-5 (Summer):2-30
      1977   *The Urban Situation*. Cambridge: MIT Press.

Chapin, F. Stuart, Jr.
      1965   *Urban Land Use Planning*. Urbana, Illinois: University
                   of Illinois Press.

Clark, Colin
      1945   "The Economic Functions of a City in Relation to
                   Its Size." *Econometrica* 13:2 (April):97-113.

Clemente, F., and R. B. Sturgis
      1971   "Population Size and Industrial Diversification."
                   Urban Studies 8:65-68.

Daly, Herman (ed.)
      1972   *Toward a Steady-State Economy*. San Francisco:
                   W. W. Freeman.

Dickerson, D. O. et al.
      1970   *Transportation Noise Pollution: Control and Abate-
                   ment*. N71-15557. Springfield, Virginia: National
                   Technical Information Service.

Duncan, Otis Dudley
      1951   "Optimum Size of Cities." In *Readings in Urban
                   Sociology*, ed. Paul K. Hatt and Albert J. Reiss, Jr.
                   Glencoe: Free Press.

Duncan, Otis Dudley, and Albert J. Reiss, Jr.
      1956   *Social Characteristics of Urban and Rural Communi-
                   ties, 1950*. New York: Wiley.

Finkler, Earl
    1972   *Nongrowth as a Planning Alternative: A Preliminary Examination of an Emerging Issue.* Washington, D.C.: American Society of Planning Officials.

Finkler, Earl, and David L. Peterson
    1974   *Nongrowth Planning Strategies: The Developing Power of Towns, Cities, and Regions.* New York: Praeger.

Fischer, Claude, Mark Baldassare, and Richard J. Ofshe
    1974   "Crowding Studies and Urban Life: A Critical Review." Working Paper 242. Berkeley: University of California, Institute of Urban and Regional Development.

Flaim, P. O.
    1968   "Jobless Trends in Twenty Large Metropolitan Areas." *Monthly Labor Review* 91:5:16–28.

Fuchs, Victor R.
    1967   "Differentials in Hourly Earnings by Region and City Size, 1959." Occasional Paper 101. New York: National Bureau of Economic Research.

Fuguitt, Glenn V., and Stanley Lieberson
    1974   "Correlations of Ratios or Difference Scores Having Common Terms." In *Sociological Methodology 1973–1974*, ed. Herbert L. Costner. Jossey-Bass.

Gold, David
    1969   "Statistical Tests and Substantive Significance." *American Sociologist* 4:1 (February): 42–46.

Gruen and Gruen Associates
    1972   *The Impacts of Growth: An Analytic Framework and Fiscal Examples.* Berkeley: California Better Housing Foundation.

Hadden, Jeffrey K., and Edgar F. Borgatta
    1965   *American Cities: Their Social Characteristics.* Chicago: Rand McNally.

Hanna, Frank A.
    1959   *State Income Differentials, 1919-1954.* Durham, North Carolina: Duke University Press.

Harvey, David
    1973   *Social Justice and the City.* Baltimore: Johns Hopkins University Press.
    1974   "Class-Monopoly Rent, Finance Capital, and the Urban Revolution." Regional Studies 8:239-55.
    1975   "The Political Economy of Urbanization in Advanced Capitalist Societies: The Case of the United States." In *The Social Economy of Cities*, ed. G. Gappert and H. Rose, pp. 129-63. Beverly Hills: Sage.

Hawley, Amos H.
    1951   "Metropolitan Population and Municipal Government Expenditures in the Central Cities." *The Journal of Social Issues*, 7:1-2, 100-8.

Hirsch, Werner, Z.
    1959   "Expenditure Implications of Metropolitan Growth and Consolidation." *Review of Economics and Statistics* 41: 232-41.
    1960   "Determinants of Public Education Expenditures." *National Tax Journal* 13:1 (March):29-40.

Hoch, Irving
    1972a   "Urban Scale and Environmental Quality." In U.S. Commission on Population Growth and the American Future, *Population, Resources and the Environment*, vol. 3. Washington, D.C.: U.S. Government Printing Office.
    1972b   "Income and City Size." *Urban Studies* 9:3 (October): 294-328.
    1976   "City Size Effects, Trends, and Policies." *Science* 193 (September):856-63.

Hoover, B. M.
    1971   *An Introduction to Regional Economics.* New York: Knopf.

International City Management Association
    1961   *Municipal Year Book.* Washington, D.C.: ICMA.
    1972   *Municipal Year Book.* Washington, D.C.: ICMA.

Jacobs, Jane
    1961   *The Death and Life of Great American Cities.* New
              York: Random House.

Johnson, D. Gale
    1952   "Some Effects of Region, Community Size, Color, and
              Occupation on Family and Individual Income." In
              Studies in Income and Wealth. Vol. 15. New York:
              National Bureau of Economic Research.

Johnson, Willard R.
    1973   "Should the Poor Buy No Growth?" *Daedelus* 102:4
              (Fall):165–89.

Kasarda, John D.
    1972   "The Impact of Suburban Population Growth on Cen-
              tral City Service Functions." *American Journal of
              Sociology* 77:6 (May):1111–24.

Kee, Woo Sik
    1967   "Suburban Population and Its Implications for Core
              City Finance." *Land Economics* 43:2 (May):202–11.

Klein, G. E. et al.
    1971   *Methods of Evaluation of the Effects of Transportation
              Systems on Community Values.* PB199-954. Spring-
              field, Virginia: National Technical Information Service.

Lamarche, Francois
    1976   "Property Development and the Economic Founda-
              tions of the Urban Question." In *Urban Sociology*, pp.
              85–118. Ed. C. C. Pickvance. New York: St. Martin's.

Levy, Steven, and Robert K. Arnold
    1972   *An Evaluation of Four Growth Alternatives in the City
              of Milpitas, 1972–1977.* Palo Alto: Institute of Re-
              gional and Urban Studies, Technical Memorandum
              Report.

Liu, Ben-Chieh
    1971   "Growth of Retail Sales, Population, and Income in
              SMSAs, 1952–1966." *Quarterly Review of Economics
              and Business* 11:2 (Summer):17–25.

Lojkine, Jean
    1976   "Contribution to a Marxist Theory of Capitalist Urban-
                ization." In *Urban Sociology*, pp. 119-46. Ed. C. G.
                Pickvance. New York: St. Martin's.

Lomax, K. S.
    1943   "The Relationship between Expenditures Per Head and
                Size of Population of County Boroughs in England and
                Wales." *Journal of the Royal Statistical Society* 106:
                1:51-59.

London County Council
    1915   *Comparative Municipal Statistics*. London: The Lon-
                don County Council.

Margolis, Julius
    1957   "Municipal Fiscal Structure in a Metropolitan Region."
                The Journal of Political Economy (June):236.

Mark, Harold, and Kent P. Schwirian
    1967   "Ecological Position, Central Place Function, and Com-
                munity Population Growth." *American Journal of So-
                ciology* 73 (July):30-41.

Meadows, Donella, Jorgen Randers, and W. W. Behrens
    1972   *The Limits to Growth*. New York: Universe Books.

Mills, Edwin S., and D. de Ferranti
    1971   "Market Choices and Optimal City Size." *American
                Economic Review* 61:2, 340-45.

Mollenkopf, John H.
    1977   "The Postwar Politics of Urban Development." In
                Cities in Change (2nd ed.), pp. 549-79. Ed. John Wal-
                ton and Donald E. Carns. Boston: Allyn and Bacon.

Molotch, Harvy
    1976   "The City as a Growth Machine." *American Journal of
                Sociology* 82:2 (September):309-32.

Morgan, James N., Ismail A. Sirageldin, and Nancy Baerwaldt
    1966   *Productive Americans*. Monograph 43. Ann Arbor:
                University of Michigan Institute for Social Research,
                Survey Research Center.

Mumford, Lewis
    1961   *The City in History: Its Origins, Its Transformations, and Its Prospects.* New York: Harcourt.

Neutze, G. M.
    1965   *Economic Policy and Size of Cities.* Canberra: Australian National University.

Nordsieck, Richard A.
    1977   *Estimates of Pollutant Emission Factors for California Motor Vehicles, 1967-2000.* RM-1849. Santa Barbara: General Research Corporation.

Ogburn, William F.
    1937   *Social Characteristics of Cities.* Chicago: International Managers' Association.

Ogburn, William F., and Otis Dudley Duncan
    1964   "City Size as a Sociological Variable." In *Contributions to Urban Sociology.* Ernest W. Burgess and Donald J. Bogue. Chicago: University of Chicago Press.

Oliver, Henry M.
    1946   "Income, Region, Community Size, and Color." *Quarterly Journal of Economics* (August):588-99.

Oxford District
    1938   A Survey of the Social Services in the Oxford District, Vol. 1: Economics and Government of a Changing Area. London: Oxford University Press.

Passel, Peter, and Leonard Ross
    1972   "Don't Know the $2-trillion Economy." *New York Times Magazine*, March 5.

Phillips, Hugh S.
    1942   "Municipal Efficiency and Town Size." *Journal of the Town Planning Institute* (May/June):139-48.

Pickvance, C. G.
    1976   *Urban Sociology.* New York: St. Martin's.

Pirages, Dennis Clark (ed.)
    1977   *The Sustainable Society: Implications for Limited Growth.* New York: Praeger.

Richardson, Harry W.
    1973   *The Economics of Urban Size.* Lexington, Mass: Lexington Books.

Samuelson, Paul A.
    1942   "The Business Cycle and Urban Development." In G. Greer (ed.), *The Problems of Cities and Towns.* Cambridge: Harvard University Press.

Schmandt, Henry J. and R. Stephens
    1963   "Local Governmental Expenditure Patterns in the United States." *Land Economics* 39:4 (November): 397-406.

Schmitt, Richard C.
    1966   "Density, Health, and Social Disorganization." *Journal of the American Institute of Planners* (January):38-40.

Schnore, Leo F.
    1963   "The Socioeconomic Status of Cities and Suburbs." *American Sociological Review* 28:1 (February):76-85.

Schnore, Leo F. and D. W. Varley
    1955   "Some Concommitants of Metropolitan Size." *American Sociological Review* 20 (August):408-14.

Schuessler, Karl
    1974   "Analysis of Ratio Variables: Opportunities and Pitfalls." *American Journal of Sociology* 80 (September): 379-96.

Scott, Stanley and E. L. Feder
    1957   *Factors Associated with Variations in Municipal Expenditure Levels.* Berkeley: University of California Bureau of Public Administration.

Shapiro, Harvey
    1963   "Economics of Scale and Local Governmental Finance." *Land Economics* 39 (May):175-86.

Shefer, D.
    1970   "Comparable Living Costs and Urban Size." *Journal of the American Institute of Planners* 36 (November): 417–21.

Sierra Club, San Diego
    1973   "Economy, Ecology, and Rapid Population Growth." San Diego California: Sierra Club of San Diego.

Smith, Brad
    1973   "A Behavioral Analysis of Questionnaire Data." PhD diss., UCSB Department of Sociology, Santa Barbara, California.

Sonquist, John, E. L. Baker, and J. N. Morgan
    1971   *Searching for Structure.* Ann Arbor Michigan: University of Michigan Institute for Survey Research.

Stanback, Thomas M. and Richard V. Knight
    1970   *The Metropolitan Economy: The Process of Employment Expansion.* New York: Columbia University Press.

Task Force on Local Government Reform
    1974   *Public Benefits from Public Choice.* Sacramento, California: State of California.

Theodoresen, George A.
    1961   *Studies in Human Ecology.* Evanston: Ron Pekerson.

Thompson, Wilbur R.
    1965   *A Preface to Urban Economics.* Baltimore: Johns Hopkins University Press, Resources for the Future.
    1968   "Internal and External Factors in the Development of Urban Economics." In *Issues in Urban Economics.* Edited by Harvey S. Perloff and London Wingo. Baltimore: Johns Hopkins University Press, Resources for the Future.
    1974   "Planning as Urban Growth Management: Still More Questions Than Answers." *A.I.P. Newsletter* 9:12 (December):7–10.

U.S. Commission on Population Growth and the American Future

1972   *Population and the American Future: The Report of the U.S. Commission on Population and the American Future.* New York: Signet.

U.S. Department of Commerce

1961a   *City Employment in 1960.* Washington, D.C.: Bureau of the Census.

1961b   *Compendium of City Government Finances in 1960.* Washington, D.C.: U.S. Government Printing Office.

1962   *County and City Data Book, 1962* (A Statistical Abstract Supplement). Washington, D.C.: U.S. Government Printing Office.

1963a   *1960 Census of Housing* (Volume I, General Housing Characteristics). Washington, D.C.: U.S. Government Printing Office.

1963b   *1960 Census of the Population* (Volume I, Number of Inhabitants and General Social and Economic Characteristics). Washington, D.C.: U.S. Government Printing Office.

1970   *City Government Finances in 1969–1970.* Washington, D.C.: U.S. Government Printing Office.

1971   *City Employment in 1970.* Washington D.C.: Bureau of the Census.

1972   *1970 Census of Housing* (Volume I, Detailed Housing Characteristics). Washington, D.C.: U.S. Government Printing Office.

1973a   *1970 Census of Population* (Volume I, Number of Inhabitants and General Social and Economic Characteristics). Washington, D.C.: U.S. Government Printing Office.

1973b   *County and City Data Book, 1972* (A Statistical Abstract Supplement). Washington, D.C.: U.S. Government Printing Office.

U.S. Department of Health, Education, and Welfare

1963   *Vital Statistics of the United States, 1960* (Volume II, Mortality, Part B). Washington, D.C.: U.S. Government Printing Office.

1973   *Vital Statistics of the United States, 1969* (Volume II, Mortality, Part B). Washington, D.C.: U.S. Government Printing Office.

U.S. Department of Justice
  1961   *Uniform Crime Reports for the United States, 1960.*
             Washington, D.C.: U.S. Government Printing Office.
  1971   *Uniform Crime Reports for the United States, 1970.*
             Washington, D.C.: U.S. Government Printing Office.

U.S. Environmental Protection Agency
  1971   *Report to the President and Congress on Noise.* December 31.

Vincent, Philip E.
  1968   "Public Expenditure Benefits and the Central City
             Exploitation Thesis." Ph.D. dissertation, Stanford
             University.

Vipond, M. J.
  1974   "City Size and Unemployment." Mimeographed.

Walker, Mabel L.
  1930   *Municipal Expenditures.* Baltimore: Johns Hopkins
             University Press.

Wallich, Henry, C.
  1972   "Zero Growth." *Newsweek*, 24 January.

Wechsler, Henry
  1961   "Community Growth, Depressive Disorders, and
             Suicide." *American Journal of Sociology* 67:1 (July):
             9–16.

Wilson, Kenneth D. (ed.)
  1977   *Prospects for Growth: Changing Expectations for the
             Future.* New York: Praeger.

RICHARD P. APPELBAUM is Assistant Professor of Sociology at the University of California, Santa Barbara. He is the author of *Theories of Social Change* (1970) and co-author of *The Effects of Urban Growth: A Population Impact Analysis* (Praeger, 1976). His articles have appeared in the *American Sociological Review*, *The American Sociologist*, *Urban Affairs Quarterly*, and elsewhere. As a member of the Santa Barbara Planning Task Force, Dr. Appelbaum was involved in studies that resulted in comprehensive growth-management measures being adopted by that city. Currently, he is actively involved in regional and local planning efforts.

RELATED TITLES
Published by
Praeger Special Studies

THE DECLINING NORTHEAST:
Demographic and Economic Analyses
edited by Benjamin Chinitz

THE EFFECTS OF URBAN GROWTH:
A Population Impact Analysis
Richard P. Appelbaum,
Jennifer Bigelow,
Henry P. Kramer,
Harvey L. Molotch, and
Paul M. Relis

EMPLOYMENT, INCOME, AND WELFARE
IN THE RURAL SOUTH
Brian Rungeling,
Lewis H. Smith,
Vernon M. Briggs, Jr., and
John F. Adams

*PROSPECTS FOR GROWTH:
Changing Expectations for the Future
edited by Kenneth D. Wilson

REGIONAL GROWTH AND DECLINE
IN THE UNITED STATES:
The Rise of the Sunbelt and the
Decline of the Northeast
Bernard L. Weinstein and
Robert E. Firestine

*THE SUSTAINABLE SOCIETY:
Implications for Limited Growth
edited by Dennis Clark Pirages

also available in paperback